SUPERNATURAL
The Unseen Powers of Animals

SUPERNATURAL

The Unseen Powers of Animals

John Downer

For my Mother

Acknowledgements

This book accompanies the BBC series *SuperNatural*. The production was a collaboration of many talents and it would be difficult to overstate the immense contribution made by every member of the production team. Producers Susan McMillan, Mark Brownlow and James Honeybourne researched and developed the main story themes. Researcher Philip Dalton unearthed many of the individual stories and Margaret Black, Nathalie Harrison and Tilly Scott-Wilson provided unfailing production support. On the practical side, Nigel Williams and Nick Pitt worked with many of the animals and film editor, Stuart Napier, crafted miles of film, shot over two years, into a coherent whole. At BBC Worldwide, Sheila Ableman, Martha Caute, Linda Blakemore and Caroline Taggart have shown great enthusiasm for the written project and produced a book of which I am proud.

SuperNatural draws on the researches of scientists across many different disciplines. Invariably our enquiries were met with invaluable suggestions and guidance, and I am indebted to everyone who gave their advice so generously. Any errors that may have crept in are entirely my own.

Lastly, I would like to thank my wife Sara for her patience at my months of absence from her life throughout this project.

This book is published to accompany the television series
SuperNatural
which was produced by John Downer Productions for the BBC Natural History Unit, Bristol, and was first broadcast on BBC 1 in 1999.
Series producer: John Downer
Producers: Susan McMillan, Mark Brownlow and James Honeybourne

Published by BBC Worldwide Ltd,
Woodlands, 80 Wood Lane, London W 12 0TT

First published 1999
© John Downer 1999
The moral right of the author has been asserted.

ISBN 0 563 38492 1

Commissioning editor: Sheila Ableman
Project editor: Martha Caute
Text editor: Caroline Taggart
Designer: Linda Blakemore
Picture researcher: Frances Abraham

Set in Cosmos by BBC Worldwide
Printed and bound in France by Imprimerie Pollina s.a.
Colour separations by Radstock Reproductions Ltd, Midsomer Norton, England
Jacket printed by Imprimerie Pollina s.a.

CONTENTS

The spectacular light
show known as the
Aurora borealis or
the northern lights is
created when high
energy particles from
the sun interact with
molecules in the Earth's
atmosphere.

There have been many books that investigate the supernatural; this one is different. It uses the latest revelations of science to investigate the truth behind the mysterious powers of animals. The word supernatural is usually applied to any powers beyond the known forces of nature, but what is known is continually being revised. New discoveries are making sense of many of the remarkable abilities of plants and animals that at one time would have been regarded as mysterious, or even paranormal. These revelations are on the cusp of present knowledge. Although many of them are astonishing, they fit credibly into the current framework of science and, in order to separate them from the purely speculative or sensational, they may perhaps be best described as SuperNatural.

The BBC TV series *SuperNatural* was inspired by a previous series, *Supersense*, which used a similar vigorous approach to explore the mysterious world of animal senses. In the ten years that have elapsed since the series was transmitted, science has not only refined many of those groundbreaking discoveries, it has also uncovered many startling new facts about animal perception. *SuperNatural* updates and reveals many of these latest findings, but its scope is far greater than that. Animals possess many hidden powers beyond the purely sensory and our new understanding of these phenomena are included here too.

At one time, all of nature was deeply mysterious and many natural events were regarded as supernatural. Birds that vanished over the winter months were a paranormal puzzle for which the only rational explanation was that they must sleep the winter away at the bottom of lakes. The thought that they might migrate to other lands was inconceivable. A similar mystery concerned the way a horse-trough would teem with life within a week of being filled with water. At the time there was only one answer – life must generate there spontaneously. No one could conceive of spores floating in the air or creatures lying in suspended animation for years.

In the past, the unexplained was so extensive that it enveloped people like a dark cloud. As increasingly accurate revelations about the powers of animals provided explanations for many previously 'supernatural' events, this cloud began to lift. But then a strange thing happened. Although more and more was being discovered, and increasing knowledge blew away much of the fog of ignorance, as the mists cleared it was found that lurking behind were even more mysteries.

Once, bats were thought of as the ultimate supernatural creature – they could mysteriously fly in complete darkness and pluck moths or other insects from the air. It occurred to nobody that they could create pictures from the echoes of their calls – their calls could not even be heard by human ears. When these amazing facts were discovered it became obvious that there were many more mysteries to be uncovered. Some moths were found to hear the bats' sonar and react by dropping out of the air; others were discovered to create jamming sounds that interfered with the bats' calls. It was then revealed that some bats avoided these counter-defences by shutting off their sonar and simply listening for the moths' wingbeats. But this was far from the limit of the new discoveries – moths were found to have sound-damping fringes on their wing-tips to avoid detection.

In other areas of research the discoveries were equally startling. At the end of the 1980s it was found that elephants communicated with sounds pitched below human hearing. Since that initial finding there has been an ever-growing list of animals shown to use this secret long-distance system of communication. In the visual arena it was revealed that the light we see is a tiny proportion of the wavelengths available to other creatures. It was also discovered that animals were endowed with many senses that had no human counterpart.

All these findings expanded our view of the natural world, pushing back the boundaries of knowledge and reducing the expanse of the supernatural realm. With growing knowledge came an increased scepticism towards old beliefs; much of what was formerly considered paranormal was dismissed as pure superstition. Recently, such scepticism has been found to be premature and many old ideas have been shown to have a basis in fact. The ancient belief in the moon's influence on the growth of plants is one such example.

In the past, people believed that crops should be planted at particular times in accordance with the phases of the moon, an idea that seemed ludicrous in the light of scientific knowledge in the early part of the twentieth century. Then, in the 1950s, a scientist discovered that the rate at which potatoes and carrots took in oxygen was related to the rising and setting of the moon; other experiments soon confirmed that plants grew better if they were sown at certain times in the moon's cycle. Recently, another scientific study confirmed the extraordinary fact that trees swell and shrink in synchrony with the moon's rhythm — it seems that, contrary to all scientific expectation, the old wisdom of folklore was right.

Just as science has difficulty coping with anything that appears irrational, it tends to ignore rarely observed events that cannot be scru-tinized by vigorous study. Some of the more baffling of these natural events include fish that fall like rain from the sky. Bizarre as it may seem, this has been observed so many times that there is little doubt that it really happens, even though the reasons remain baffling.

Science is still searching for answers in whole areas of the natural world. Even after decades of research, the means animals use to navigate across the globe is an area of fierce debate. Some of the most exciting developments concern the powers of animals at the extremes of existence, some buried many kilometres under the Earth. These organisms, which are able to tolerate extremes of heat and pressure and subsist on nothing but rock, are providing insights into the possible characteristics of life on other planets.

As it charts the latest discoveries, *SuperNatural* treads the thin line between scientific knowledge and the unexplained; where possible, it offers credible scientific explanations of what could be happening, but sometimes the reasons are simply not known. In time, these ideas will become refined or revised in a process that pushes back the boundaries of the mysterious world once known as the supernatural.

John Downer

1

EXTRASENSORY PERCEPTION

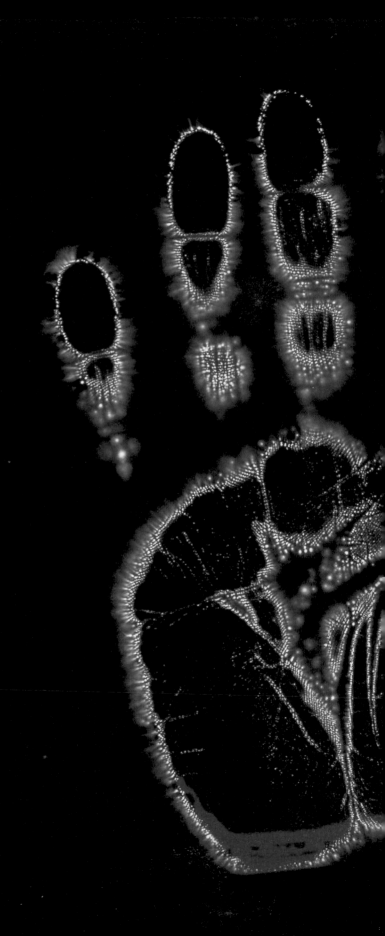

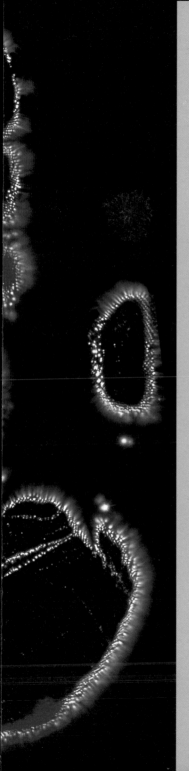

Occasionally we catch glimpses of a world outside our normal sensory realm; we may feel a presence, predict an event or simply sense something that makes us feel uneasy. At these times our senses are driven into overload, our perception becomes super-sensitized and we are primed to respond to the slightest sign of danger. When we lived among wild animals these feelings would have been common – they were the key to our survival. Our sense organs, reacting at the limits of their abilities, would send out a subconscious warning that danger was lurking not far away.

In nature, the same reactions happen every day. A stalking lion is often sensed by its potential prey long before it is seen. A frisson of nervousness ripples through the herd – they know that danger is out there…

Today our sense organs are rarely called upon to save our lives and such moments of SuperNatural perception are rare. But animals spend their lives in this heightened world and, what is more, they have senses that almost defy human belief. For them, extrasensory perception is a daily reality.

Consider the functioning of any human sense and its limitations soon become only too apparent. Vision, our primary sense, depends on analysing how objects reflect light. But the light we perceive is only a tiny sample of the electromagnetic waves that rain down on us. Beyond visible light, at the high-frequency end of the spectrum, are ultraviolet waves; beyond these are X-rays and further again are cosmic rays. Below visible light, at the low-frequency end of the scale, are infrared waves, followed by microwaves and radio waves. Although our unaided eyes tune into only a narrow band of this available information, many creatures perceive far more.

Our hearing is similarly limited; we can detect sound waves only when they vibrate above twenty times and below 20,000 times a second. Some animals hear sounds pitched ten times higher than this, while others hear them pitched eight times lower. All our senses suffer from the same severe restrictions.

This may seem humbling enough, but there are some creatures that experience the world through senses we can only imagine. Think how the world would appear if it were made visible purely by the way it conducted electricity or reflected water ripples and you gain a sense of the bizarre possibilities. Although we share the same planet, these creatures have a SuperNatural view of reality which bears little resemblance to our own.

Science is continually gaining insights into the hidden sensory powers of animals. Each discovery allows us to glimpse another way of perceiving the world. What it reveals is the extraordinary truth behind animal ESP.

Auras

Psychics maintain that every living thing has an aura. These glowing emanations, which are supposed to suffuse and surround the body, respond to emotional states and give an indication of health. In 1939 a Russian scientist accidentally discovered he could photograph what appeared to be an aura. He placed his hand on a photographic plate and passed a high-voltage electrical discharge through it; when the film was developed, an eerie firework display of colour outlined the imprint of a hand. He soon found that any living organism created the same spooky impression in a process that came to be known as Kirlian photography.

The most impressive auras were those produced by leaves that had a part freshly cut away. The photographic imprint showed not only the outline of the leaf but also that of the missing part. This ghostly impression was thought to prove the existence of a supernatural spirit that overlaid the physical body of any living organism.

More vigorous scientific research dampened early enthusiasm for the new discoveries. The Kirlian 'aura' could be explained by electrical discharges creating ionization effects around the objects which were then recorded on the film; the phantom leaf seemed to be the result of contamination left on the photographic plate. Most scientists no longer believe in the significance of the Kirlian effect, although it has some Russian advocates who claim it can be used as a diagnostic tool in medicine. So, given these setbacks, does an aura really exist?

All living organisms hum with electromagnetic radiation that extends beyond their purely physical body and this is an aura in all but name. Our limited senses cannot detect most of these emanations, but some creatures are exquisitely sensitive to them.

Like all warm-blooded creatures humans glow like a light bulb with the electromagnetic rays we know as heat. We can see this thermal aura only through thermographic cameras which display variations of body temperature as differing colours. Our hot cheeks show up as fiery red, our cooler nose and earlobes a mellow orange or yellow and our cold hair and fingernails an icy blue.

Medical thermographic cameras are so sensitive that they can be used to detect the raised temperatures caused by arthritis and even tumours. Their use in modern medicine has an intriguing connection. Of all creatures, snakes have the longest association with the medical profession – a creature that could kill so easily was also believed to possess life-giving powers, and its capacity for rebirth, shown by its shedding of its skin, confirmed its powers of rejuvenation. The Greek god of medicine, Aesculapius, always had snakes in attendance and was supposed to be able to transform himself into a serpent at will; even today, the emblem of the medical profession features entwined serpents. And we now know that some snakes possess powers that surpass the best thermographic cameras.

The heat-imaging system of some snakes may not be used for medical diagnosis but, like the cameras in hospital, it analyses living bodies. Snakes use their thermographic technique to track down prey. Two rival designs have evolved: the pit vipers, such as rattlesnakes and copperheads, have a single heat-sensitive pit on either side of the head just behind the nostrils; the boids, a group which includes the boa constrictor, the python and the anaconda, have an array of up to thirteen. Each pit acts like an eye, but one that focuses heat rather than light. Instead of a retina, the image falls on a grid of 7000 nerve endings which are so sensitive that they can detect a change of

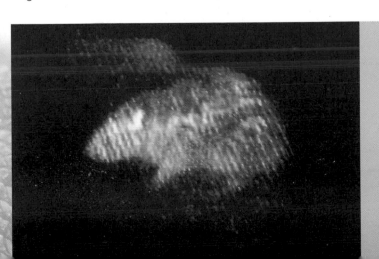

Far left The two pit organs just below the rattlesnake's eyes gather a heat image of its prey and guide its deadly strike.

Left This image from an infrared photograph of a rat shows how the snake would see its prey.

Below The most impressive auras created by Kirlian photography were those of leaves which had part of them freshly cut away. The photographic image showed not only the remaining leaf but the missing part as well.

Opposite Like the pit organs of a snake, the thermographic camera is sensitive to tiny variations of temperature on the surface of the skin. It is used by doctors to detect diseases and abnormalities, such as arthritis and tumours.

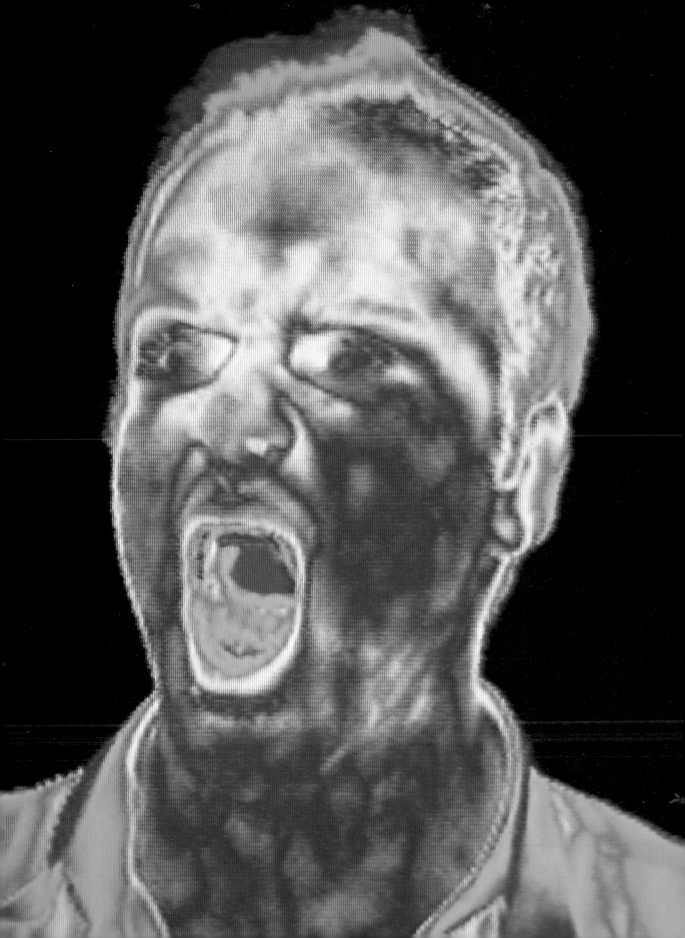

as little as 0.003°C. They react faster than any thermographic camera and will register a change of temperature in just a 35-thousandth of a second.

The pit organs lack the resolution of normal vision, but they can easily discern the heat aura of a snake's victim in total darkness. They can even see the ghostly trace left by warm footprints. When they do find their prey, additional heat sensors in the mouth guide the final deadly strike.

Other predators, such as the legendary vampire, have also discovered the grisly value of tuning into body heat. Like the python, the vampire bat has truly SuperNatural powers. The strange, convoluted area of skin that adorns its nose is a heat-guidance system tuned in to the warmth of its victim's blood. This nose leaf is shielded by insulating tissue from the bat's own body heat and has a temperature 9°C lower. It is exquisitely sensitive to other sources of heat, particularly those radiating from another animal's blood-filled tissues, so, when the bat is near its prey, the nose leaf guides the bat in towards the most nourishing parts of its meal.

The convoluted nose leaf of the vampire bat is a sense organ tuned to the warmth emanating from the blood-filled tissues of its prey. It guides the bat in the final attack.

All Electric

Living processes give off other kinds of auras besides heat. The most universal are those created by electricity. Like all living organisms we pulse with electricity; our every thought, every muscular action creates a corresponding electrical storm of minute currents. It is difficult for a land-living creature to detect an electric aura because air acts as an insulator, preventing our nervous discharges leaking into the outside world, but in water things are very different. Electricity readily leaks out of the body into this natural conductor, giving off an array of signals. Consequently, creatures that can sense electricity are all aquatic; among them are the ocean's most ferocious predators.

Sharks and rays are masters at detecting body electricity. They use jelly-filled tubes called the ampullae of Lorenzini to find their prey. These deathly sensors are dotted around the shark's head and also sunk in canals running the length of its body. They are so receptive that they can detect discharges as low as a 20-billionth of a volt, which is equivalent to sensing the voltage flowing between the terminals of a 1.5-volt battery placed 3000 kilometres apart in the sea. So how do they fare when sensing the body electricity of a human body?

As we swim, our skin acts like a giant layer of insulation tape, preventing most of our telltale electrical aura from reaching the water. But where the body opens to the outside world electricity seeps from every orifice, creating fields ranging from 1/10,000,000 to 1/100,000,000 of a volt. Fortunately, this leaking electricity quickly dissipates, so even the hypersensitive shark has to be under a metre away to detect these fields. But if we are injured, tears in the insulating layer of skin allow electricity to pour into the water, guiding a shark from 3 metres away. The shark's electro-sensors not only help it find living food, they also guide the final attack when the shark's mouth is open and its vision is obscured.

Luckily for us, sharks have an array of other senses, giving them an acute sensitivity to smell, sound and visual signals. They are also choosy eaters and, as humans are not their favourite food, when we feature on their menu, it is usually by mistake.

Stingrays use their electric sense for finding food hidden beneath the sand and, like their prey, they also hide themselves in this way. But the males can use their electric sense to distinguish the electrical auras of hidden females and they use this knowledge to track down a suitable mate.

Sharks, rays and skates belong to an ancient group of cartilaginous (non-bony) fish known as the Elasmobranchs. Their antiquity suggests that the electric sense has been around for a long time. Just how long was revealed when another type of fish, the prehistoric Coelacanth, present 500 million years ago, was rediscovered alive in the catch of a South African fishing trawler in 1938. It too had electro-receptors. As more discoveries are made it seems that the value of finding prey

Right Our skin acts as an insulator preventing most of our body electricity escaping into the water. Even so, a shimmer of electricity surrounds us like an aura.

Opposite Sharks can only sense this electricity when very close. But if a cut rips through the body's insulation, electricity bleeds into the water reaching a shark as much as 3 metres away.

by tuning into its body electricity has made electro-sensing widespread among aquatic hunters.

Two groups of freshwater fish also use electro-sensing, as do the tadpoles of many amphibians; electro-sensing hairs have also recently been discovered on the cuticle of crayfish. There is even a mammal with these powers. The Australian platypus's bizarre duck-like bill is studded with electro-sensors that can detect voltages as low as one 500-millionth of a volt. It hunts freshwater shrimps that are often hidden in the murky water, but as the shrimp flick their tails trying to escape they send out a thousandth-of-a-volt 'come and get me' signal a metre into the water.

Electric Force Fields

The human body's life processes create only weak electric auras, but imagine a creature that not only generates a high-voltage aura but can use it to sense the world. Such powers may seem to surpass the paranormal but, remarkably, such a creature exists. In fact, two groups of freshwater fish have independently evolved

these incredible abilities. They are the Mormyriformes of Africa and the Gymnotiformes of South America.

These fish create electric fields using generators derived from modified muscles or nerve cells, stacked like batteries along the fish's body. When they discharge, an electric force field of between 1 and 10 volts radiates from head to tail. As the fish swims, this field is warped by the electrical conductivity of the surroundings. The fish monitors these fluctuations by means of thousands of special sensors along its body and uses the information to create an electric image.

What an electric fish perceives depends on how readily its surroundings allow current to flow. Rocks would appear as dark shapes because their insulating properties act as a barrier to the electrical force field. Plants, with their greater conductivity, would suck in the field, making them appear brighter, while metal objects would dazzle like a glowing light bulb.

This alien view has another bizarre characteristic. Because the force field is not continuous but fired at intervals, it creates instantaneous snapshots of the world as though frozen in a photographer's flash. In addition, by raising the pulse frequency,

The electric eel creates a force field around itself and senses the world by detecting disturbances in the field.

like a strobe light at a rave, the fish 'sees' an increasingly speedily sampled view.

African electric fish sample the world just once every 20 seconds, so they are effectively experiencing a power cut for most of the time. But the South American species fire their field around 50 times each second, creating a near-continuous picture.

As well as being useful for navigation, electric imaging can be used for hunting. The black ghost knife fish, native to the turbid waters of the Amazon basin, uses its electric field to find plankton. It swims backwards, tail first, scanning its prey like a bar-code reader until its mouth is within grabbing distance of its prey.

Electrical imaging systems like these work only at close range – anything more than a metre away simply vanishes in a fog of electrical noise.

Death Rays

Some fish have taken electric generation to its shocking conclusion. The torpedo ray generates 2 kilowatts of power at 220 volts which it uses on both predators and prey. This is the equivalent of momentarily dropping a two-bar electric heater into the water and the result is that its victim is stunned and sent into spasms. The South American electric eel is another shocker; the 800 volts of electricity it can discharge are enough to kill a horse.

Other animals might not be as stunningly dramatic as the electric eel, but all of them use electricity in some way. Our every thought is accompanied by electrical discharges, as are the nervous impulses of other animals. But do plants react in the same way? Recent evidence suggests that they may.

Sensitive Plants

If you could speed up time and watch the clematis in your garden grow, it would appear almost sentient, its growing tip twirling and exploring, searching sensitively for support. When its tendrils touched something they would send out an electrical signal like the nervous impulses of an animal. The immediate result would be changes to the growth plan of the tendril, causing it to curl into a spring and then contract, securing the plant. Because plants live in a different time world to us we are largely unaware of how sensitive they are. Perhaps it is just as well.

When we cut the grass it screams – not with a voice, but with electricity. The severed tips indicate their distress by sending electrical signals to the base of the stem.

Because plants lack the specialized nerve cells of animals the message is carried a thousand times slower than it would be in the nervous system of an animal, but electricity still flows between cells and the plant still reacts. The base of the stem responds as if grazing animals were eating the grass blades and it reacts by producing poisons followed by a spurt of new growth. Soon, the lawnmower has to be used again.

Take a Strimmer to a bed of stinging nettles and the reaction is even more dramatic. New growth soon erupts from the wounded stems, but this time the thorns are stronger, more numerous and vicious. They have grown back with a vengeance.

If plants are so sensitive, can we affect their growth just by talking to and caressing them? Very possibly we can. Whenever we stroke a plant, channels in the cells that are sensitive to stretching send an electrical signal ordering it to manufacture the building materials lignin and cellulose. Within 15–20 minutes of this first caress, the plant hormone ethylene seeps out of pores and wafts over the plant, stimulating cells and controlling their growth.

Houseplants are sensitive to a caring touch because we imprison them in unnatural conditions, sheltered from the daily stimulation they receive in the wild. Protected from the normal buffeting of wind, they become ultra-sensitive to any attention they may receive from us. Our caress is a welcome substitute for wild stimulation from wind and the result is a bushier, healthier plant.

The heightened sensitivity of houseplants to vibration seems to extend the stimulation created by loud sounds. High frequencies, such as that of human conversation, appear slightly to increase living rates and to promote growth. Some music has a similar positive effect, but plants appear to like only certain kinds. They have refined tastes, responding well to classical piano music but hating the bass notes of heavy metal or rap. These bad vibes seem to inhibit photosynthesis (the process by which plants manufacture food) and close the plant's pores, causing it to react as though it had been exposed to strong winds. Prolonged exposure to loud music causes even greater damage: the stems thicken and, in extreme cases, the leaves drop off. The worst place for a plant is a teenager's bedroom!

Another effect of talking to plants may be even better for them – our breath is food. Plants need carbon dioxide for photosynthesis and, because they evolved in an era when carbon dioxide levels were far higher than today, they are now gasping for a fix. Talking to plants can increase concentrations of this gas up to 200 times. Lighting gas or coal fires, having friends around or keeping pets creates an even stronger effect and carbon dioxide levels in such socially enriched households may reach a thousand times those found outside. Plants love every breath of it.

Talking Plants

Although plants benefit from our words, we can be sure that no plant really understands them. But some plants do something almost as SuperNatural — they communicate with their neighbours.

In Africa, when giraffes or other browsers eat acacia trees, the newly munched leaves send out a chemical SOS to the rest of the tree. Within 30 minutes, concentrations of bitter-tasting tannins in the leaves may have doubled; to avoid being poisoned, the animal has to move away. But nearby acacias are off limits as well.

Their leaves have received the wind-borne message and they have increased their tannin concentrations to toxic levels too.

To cope with these plant defences, antelope and other grazers feed for only a short time before seeking new pastures. The natural value of this fastidiousness was proved when a herd of kudu was fenced in with an acacia stand as its only source of food. All the antelope mysteriously died. The post-mortem revealed liver poisoning due to an over-consumption of tannin – the leaves they had been forced to eat showed toxic concentrations three times higher than normal.

Although such communication between plants may seem remarkable, it is now known that some plants do some-thing far more extraordi-nary – they actually send distress calls to insects.

Our garden beans may appear defenceless against an invasion of green-fly, but left to its own devices the plant has a remarkable solution. It produces a chemical SOS that wafts across suburbia, summoning a defence force of the aphid's enemies. Soon squadrons of parasitic wasps descend to lay their eggs inside the aphids' bodies. When the eggs hatch, the grubs consume their host while it is still alive.

Other plants, including cotton and maize, have discovered the benefits of summoning these deadly aerial squadrons. Maize plants are so sophisticated at identifying their foes that they can distinguish the ages of the caterpillars that prey on them. They send out an emergency call to the parasitic wasps only if they are attacked by young caterpillars, as these have a lifetime of damage still ahead of them.

Opposite Acacia trees attacked by grazers, such as giraffes (below), send out a chemical SOS; when neighbouring trees receive the wind-borne signal, they react by increasing the toxins in their leaves.

This 5-metre-high architectural wonder was made by termites. Secret chemical messages from the maggot-like queen and in the saliva of the workers controlled the insect construction team.

Scent Sense

Because our sense of smell is so poor we are only dimly aware of this world of chemical signals and scents. But, for other life, its significance is overwhelming.

Our nasal membrane covers about 4 square centimetres, a dog's may cover 150. Such a discrepancy is a clue to the vast amount of olfactory information that simply wafts unnoticed through our lives. Many animals tune in to this chemical world and show feats of olfactory perception that almost defy belief.

A bloodhound is a million times more sensitive to human scent than we are. A shark can sense a litre of blood dissolved in a billion litres of water. Emperor moths detect the alluring scent of a female from 5 kilometres away. Polar bears can smell a seal colony from a distance of 30 kilometres. These feats only hint at a hidden world. All around the air is filled with the secret chemical messages of other creatures. For many communally living animals, odours are so important they almost totally control their lives.

The incredible organization of a termite colony was once assumed to involve some kind of telepathic communication. How else could the thousands of individuals work as a team and construct the architectural wonders that make up their homes, complete with sophisticated refinements such as cooling chimneys and an air-conditioning system? It is now known that the feat of organization is achieved by smell messages. At the command centre of the nest is a single, huge, maggot-like queen whose odours pervade the entire colony. Her scent even dictates the exact dimensions of the chamber that the workers construct around her. Her smell messages also stimulate the workers to tend and feed her and prevent them developing ovaries. As the workers build the colony, using millions of tiny gobbets of saliva and mud, they lay down a scent message that guides the other workers to follow the same construction plan.

Bees and ants use smell in a similar SuperNatural way to control the complexities of the organizations that make up their colonies. At one time this sophisticated use of smell was believed to be solely the preserve of social insects, but it has recently been discovered that the strange subterranean mammal known as the naked mole rat organizes its life in a similar way.

Bee Vision

As well as possessing a heightened sense of smell, many animals also see in a way that is totally different to ours. We see in colour because different light-sensitive cones in our eyes respond to red, green and blue wavelengths of light. Bees also have three colour receptors to give them full-colour vision, but they see the world differently. One of their receptors is sensitive to ultraviolet (UV) light – a wavelength that we simply cannot see – and, in turn, bees cannot see red; to them it would appear black. In effect the whole of their vision is shifted away from the red end of the spectrum towards ultraviolet, giving them a totally different perception of colour. If we were to perceive the world as bees do, as well as seeing the eerie glow of ultraviolet light, we would find that familiar colours such as purple were replaced by the baffling mix of ultraviolet and yellow known as 'bee's purple'. Overlaying many of these colours would be patterns that had previously been invisible. Flowers would reveal strange markings and the sky would display concentric patterns. We humans cannot see the ultraviolet waves that make these signals visible, but many creatures do peer into this hidden world.

Deadly Rays

Some ultraviolet light is dangerous to human health. The shorter wavelengths of this invisible band of light can destroy the genetic code in our cells and also promote cancers. As a defence our skin produces a protective screen of a pigment called melanin, giving us a suntan as a by-product; we increase this natural protection by using sunscreen lotion. Sunglasses help prevent these dangerous rays reaching our sensitive retina, but they simply supplement the UV blocking filters already installed in our lens and cornea.

Amazingly many creatures can cope with the harmful effects of ultraviolet. They even use the less harmful wavelengths as a major source of illumination.

Because many insects see ultraviolet, flowers use secret markings in this colour to attract insect pollinators. Floral decorations, invisible to human eyes, guide insects such as butterflies and bees to the nectar and pollen at the centre of the flower.

A host of other creatures have recently been shown to see this eerie light. They include mantis shrimps, horseshoe crabs, many reptiles and amphibians, as well as squid and octopus. Of the recent discoveries, one of the most intriguing was the sensitivity shown by coral fish – they shimmer with colours we can only imagine. Equally surprising was the degree to which birds use ultraviolet light.

The plumage of many birds sparkles with hidden ultraviolet signals. Even familiar birds such as starlings use UV as a lighting effect in their plumage and females choose males with the most alluring ultraviolet shimmer. More exotically, parrots, cassowaries and zebra finches all have ultraviolet plumage patterns. These signals are so important that, when a male bluethroat had an ultraviolet block applied experimentally to his plumage, he immediately lost his attractiveness to the opposite sex, even though the visible colours were unaffected. Older birds tend to reflect ultraviolet most, and these more experienced birds also have the most success in courtship.

Left Close-up of a peacock feather. A peacock's display is spectacular to our vision, but to creatures that can see ultraviolet light it must present an even more dazzling display. Many birds use these secret signals to select a mate.

Above A hovering kestrel can see the urine trails of its prey (left) by the way the stain absorbs ultraviolet light, probably seeing the runs as yellow traces. This might help it to decide where to hunt.

To enable them to detect UV, birds have an extra colour cone in their eye. In addition, they can see the same range of colours that we can and this must give them an incredibly enhanced impression of the world. If we were endowed with a bird's eye, colours would not only appear far more saturated or intense, they would also change hue depending on how they absorbed or reflected ultraviolet. As parts of our body reflected this light we would start to look different. Our hair would shimmer with a ghostly UV glow and our nails would seem to be painted with iridescent varnish. As we applied clear suntan lotion to our bodies, to block out ultraviolet rays, we would shift the familiar colour spectrum and appear as though smeared with yellow cream.

Besides making us look weirdly colourful and a bird's plumage even more spectacular, the unique characteristics of UV light help birds to find food. The waxy coatings on seeds, fruits and berries all reflect ultraviolet. So, against the dark background of a hedgerow, blackberries and other fruits shine out like beacons to foraging birds. The shiny waxy cuticles of insects also sparkle with ultraviolet, attracting insect-eaters such as robins and wrens; similarly, caterpillars camouflaged to human eyes against a leafy green background become luminously visible to blue-tits and other predators.

Even birds of prey may benefit from this light fantastic. Voles mark their runs with scent trails of urine. Although this maze of secret pathways is normally invisible, because they absorb ultraviolet light they become conspicuous to birds. A foraging kestrel can therefore monitor a vole's movements and concentrate hunting where activity is greatest.

Guiding Light

For a light we cannot see and one so potentially harmful to us, it is remarkable how vital ultraviolet is to most of the natural world. It is even used as an aid to navigation. When light leaves the sun, the light waves vibrate in all possible directions, but when these chaotic rays collide with the atmosphere, a strange thing happens: they become organized and made to vibrate in the same direction. This polarized light is invisible to us, but it forms concentric patterns in the sky that many animals can use for navigation. These markings indicate the sun's position even when it is obscured by cloud. Bees, desert ants and many other insects are all known to read this sky map and it now seems that birds may follow it too. Shorter wavelengths of light, such as ultraviolet, are most readily polarized, so being able to see these wavelengths gives the navigators a great advantage. In the ocean, this sky map could be visible, at ultraviolet wavelengths, as deep as 600 metres and fish, which can see ultraviolet, may refer to it on their migrations.

Far-red Vision

As well as seeing ultraviolet, some fish can see far-red, a wavelength beyond the other limit of our visual spectrum. Although we cannot see it, we have turned this handicap to our advantage by using far-red to control much of our modern technology. Unlike us, a goldfish in a living room sees the remote-control beams that change channels on the TV or work the hi-fi. A goldfish kept in a security hut would even see the security lights, invisible to us, that are used for camera surveillance.

This power to see far-red light developed in the murky water of the goldfish's original home. Here, water coloured black by organic decay absorbs almost all light except far-red. Although these dim waters appear impenetrable to our eyes, to a goldfish far-red light shafts through like a spotlight.

The masters of far-red vision are piranhas; these razor-toothed predators of South America can use their penetrating eyesight to single out a victim through the inky blackness of the Amazon and strip it to the bone within minutes.

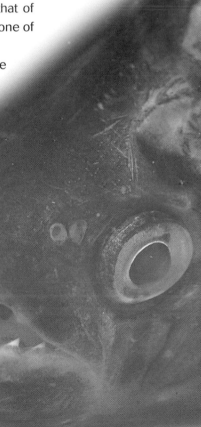

The piranha can see far-red light, invisible to human eyes. This allows its eyes to pierce the murky waters of the Amazon and seek out its prey.

Ripple Sense

Besides having a different visual system from that of other creatures, fish also have another sense – one of the strangest in the animal world.

For us, water is the most alien environment and it is here that one of the most bizarre of all sensory systems is found. Imagine entering this watery world and sensing your surroundings entirely by the way they reflected ripples. This strange method of imaging is found among several aquatic creatures, but fish have perfected it. They use sensors, consisting of sensitive hairs attached to jelly-like rods, to detect water movement. These neuromasts, as they are called, come in two models. The cruder versions are free-standing organs widely distributed over the fish's body; the more refined are sunk into protective channels, known as lateral lines, and these sense the outside world through pores. The lateral line runs the length of the fish's body and is so sophisticated that it can actually gather an image of the outside environment. It does this in a remarkable way.

As the fish swims, water flowing around its body creates a continuous wake, like the bow wave of a ship. Nearby objects reflect this wave back and, like a wave hitting a shore, the returning ripples arrive along the body at slightly different times. The

Like most fish, the flamboyant Siamese fighting fish uses its ripple sense to detect the world. When danger threatens, the male fish trembles his fins to send a ripple warning to his brood. They react by hiding in his mouth.

lateral line analyses these time differences and from this information the fish creates an image of its surroundings based on how they reflect back its bow wave. The fish gains greater resolution simply by swimming faster and creating more ripples.

The system can be astonishingly detailed; the Mexican blind cave fish relies entirely on its lateral line for imaging in the darkness of the cave; even without eyes it can still perceive objects smaller than a pinhead.

Going with the Flow

Over 25,000 different fish species have some version of the lateral line system and they use it for many purposes besides imaging. Schooling fish use their lateral line to monitor their whereabouts within a shoal and co-ordinate movements with their neighbours. Trout maintain their position in a rapidly flowing river by using it to detect the way a boulder distorts the water flow.

Even simple neuromasts, not arranged into a sophisticated lateral line, still have extraordinary powers. Using an array of neuromasts on its head, the common minnow can accurately home in on floundering insects at the water's surface. Siamese fighting fish have even developed a ripple alarm system. In this liberated species it is the male who tends the brood of up to 150 offspring. When danger threatens he trembles his pectoral fins and calls to his young with ripples. They react by swimming towards him. He then accomplishes a vanishing trick by sucking them

The magical synchronization of a shoal of fish can be explained by each fish's lateral line sensing the movements of its neighbour. By making instant adjustments all the fish are able to swirl in sympathy.

into his mouth. Once danger has passed he regurgitates them unharmed.

In water the ripple sense is so useful that many other water-living organisms have developed their own versions. The tadpoles of many amphibians image the world through free-standing water sensors, while octopus and squid have a similar simple system of free-standing hairs on their many arms.

Winds of Change

Just as some aquatic creatures discern their world through water movement, those on land or in the air need to sense air movements.

Birds keep track of shifting air currents using modified feathers known as filo-plumes. These hair-like feathers lie alongside each contour feather (the main large feathers of the wings and tail) and monitor their movements. As well as assessing air currents they also tell the bird whether its plumage needs preening, an essential aspect of keeping itself clean and healthy.

A spider's hairy legs contain specialist hairs sensitive to the slightest breath of wind. Scorpions have similar hairs, called trichobothria hairs, on their legs and pincers. A breeze whispering along at just 0.072 kilometres per hour can cause these hairs to sway, so the wings of flying insects waft a powerful warning of their approach. Cockroaches keep their air-detecting hairs on two finger-like organs that project from the back of their body. So sensitive are they that they can even detect the air current created from the footfalls of another cockroach. The hurricane-force signals sent by a human footstep allow them to vanish the moment we enter a room.

As well as air-sensing trichobothria, tarantulas and other spiders also have organs that sense ground vibrations. Drum-like membranes, stretched over slits in the animal's cuticle, pick up the tiny tremors created by the movement of their prey. Under good conditions they can sense prey 10 metres away.

Thumping Elephants

It has recently been discovered that elephants also sense vibrations but, in keeping with their immense size, the distances involved are scaled accordingly.

Folklore has endowed elephants with the SuperNatural ability to communicate with each other over many kilometres of open bush. Anecdotal accounts suggest that elephants know if danger threatens another distant herd. Many of these stories come from culling programmes where the time a herd was killed coincided with distress shown in another herd some way away. These stories have always tended to be treated with scepticism, but recent discoveries seem to provide an intriguing explanation.

When elephants are threatened they thump the ground in mock charges. The ground literally shakes under their thunderous stomping. But it seems that rather than simply induging in a fit of intimidating temper, the elephants may also be sending a message, as the tremors may carry for 50 kilometres.

This feat is possible because the ground transmits vibration far more efficiently than air. Another elephant could tune in to these distant signals, just as it is possible to hear a distant train by putting an ear to the rail. But instead of lying with its

Opposite A spider's legs are covered by wind-sensing hairs known as trichobothria. These are responsive to the slightest breath of air and can be used to detect the movements of predators and prey.

Left Elephants were the first land animals shown to communicate with infrasounds pitched below human hearing. Recently, another long-distance communication system used by animals has been discovered — one based on earth tremors.

huge ear to the ground, the elephant uses its gigantic feet as vibration detectors. The tremor simply passes through the front legs up into the ear. Because each leg receives the vibration with a slightly different time lag an elephant could use this information to work out the direction of the stomping.

Before this discovery was made, an equally startling revelation had found another secret communication system among elephants. This used sound pitched below human hearing.

Calling Long Distance

Low-frequency sound penetrates further than high frequencies. This is why the thumping bass of a neighbour's stereo is so irritating even though the tune is too quiet to be recognized. Sound pitched below the limits of our hearing carries even further. These penetrating sound waves, below 20 cycles per second (20 hertz or Hz), are known as infrasound.

Elephants create and hear these secret sounds. They use their foreheads as huge sounding boards to transmit infrasonic rumbles over vast distances. An elephant can eavesdrop on another 4 kilometres away, covering an area around 50 square kilometres. At dusk, because of the change in the acoustic properties of the air, the range increases dramatically, enabling the elephant to extend its social networking to a neighbourhood of 300 square kilometres. Thus distant herds may be reunited and lone males can find females.

The fact that elephants communicate with infrasound was a landmark discovery. Since then a surprising range of animals have been shown to have this ability.

The hippo's booming sarcastic-sounding bellow, as loud as a heavy metal band, vibrates any creature less than 15 metres away. It has just been discovered that an infrasonic rumble precedes this earth-shaking audible sound, travelling as much as 30 kilometres through the water. A huge larynx produces this deep baritone, which either passes out of the nostrils into the air or is transmitted through the blubbery throat tissue into the water. Hippos hear the airborne sounds though their external ears, but the waterborne sound passes to the internal ear through the jaw. As sound travels faster in water than in air, hippos may use the time lag of the airborne sound to judge distances.

When a rhino is enraged it bellows with the kind of prehistoric calls that we might imagine dinosaurs to have made. These resonating sounds are now known to have infrasonic components. When danger threatens, the mother uses these low-pitched warnings to call protectively to her offspring.

The okapi, a weird, horned, forest-dwelling relative of the giraffe, is another low-pitched caller, barking at frequencies between 7 and 25 hertz. In dense bush,

Rhinos are among the many animals now known to communicate with sound pitched below the hearing range of humans.

Hippos have been shown to have a secret underwater communication system and their bellows also contain infrasonic waves that can carry along a river for 30 kilometres.

infrasound helps an okapi keep in contact with other members of its herd. Females also make infrasonic sounds to advertise their reproductive condition and later to call to their calves. This secret communication system not only allows okapi to call long distance; it also enables them to converse without attracting the attentions of their main predator, the leopard.

When it was discovered that okapis produced infrasound, investigations into their nearest relative the giraffe began. Infrasonic recordings soon revealed a private communication system in an animal formerly thought to be mute.

As well as an increasing number of mammals, reptiles, such as crocodiles and alligators, have also been discovered using infrasound. Male alligators are the most spectacular performers. They boom out their courtship calls and the alligator with the deepest roar gets the girl. If they call while in the water the sounds become visual signals, too, as the vibrations create a spectacular dance of water at the surface.

A variety of birds have also been shown to have infrasonic components in their calls, including the capercallie, kori bustard, prairie chickens and many kinds of pigeon. Birds also hear the deepest infrasounds of any animal, which may give them remarkable extrasensory abilities.

Sound Bearings

Some migrating birds travel long distances by exploiting thermals – the vortexes of rising air that form over sun-baked ground. By spiralling up in these invisible elevators, soaring birds such as storks, cranes and pelicans gain enough height to glide for hundreds of metres with scarcely a wingbeat. Provided they can find another thermal at the end of their glide, they have the means for almost effortless intercontinental flight. Fortunately for them, thermals create a roar of infrasound, which they can hear 3 kilometres away. Although not all migrating birds use thermals, these low-frequency sounds may help them in other ways, too.

Walk away from the sea and the rhythmic swell of the surf can be heard far from the shore. But at a distance, all the high frequencies are absorbed and the sea wash becomes a low roar. Still further way, the sounds drop so low in pitch that they vanish altogether. If we had the acute hearing of a bird, although the sounds would continue to decrease in pitch, they could still be heard even hundreds of kilometres away.

This incredible range is possible because birds hear extreme infrasound (as low as one cycle every ten seconds). At these frequencies sound travels almost unhindered. Besides the infrasound of the ocean, other remote sound sources become audible too – wind on mountain ranges and the whispering sands of the desert.

If migrating birds listened to the changing patterns of these distant sound sources they could use them as acoustic beacons to keep track of their journey.

Fish also detect infrasound, so migratory species such as salmon and cod may conceivably listen to underwater infrasound to navigate. As on land, the deep ocean provides several constant sources of infrasound. As well as waves, turbulence due to ocean currents and seismic motions of the sea floor all create deep sound sources which fish could use to gain their bearings.

Transatlantic Calling

Several types of whale, including the largest creature on earth, the blue whale, use infrasound of around 20 hertz to call long distance. They are helped by the fact that water carries sound quickly and efficiently, meaning that calls can be heard hundreds of kilometres away. They are also aided by a phenomenon so useful it was once a military secret.

In water the speed of sound varies with temperature, salinity and pressure and at depths of around 1500 metres these factors combine to form a channel which acts like a voice tube, allowing almost unbelievable distances to be bridged. This secret channel has been used by the military for years and at the end of the Cold War it was revealed that whales were using this clandestine communication channel too. They used it to call across oceans.

Whales can communicate over extreme distances, but they still face a problem. Although sound travels five times faster in water than in air, even at speeds of 1.5 kilometres a second it would still take a whale one hour to communicate from London to New York, a distance of 5400 kilometres. If the distances are so great and the time delays so large, what on earth can whales be saying that might be significant?

As usual sex might provide an answer. Despite intensive efforts by whalers, the breeding grounds of the low-voiced whales have never been found. Perhaps the calls allow them to make secret trysts somewhere in the deep ocean.

Another intriguing possibility is that they call to each other when they find shoals of krill, the tiny marine creatures that make up the bulk of their diet. But as any whale receiving the message might have to travel over 5000 kilometres to feed on these tiny crustaceans, is there any point to their communication? Making the journey presents no problem – whales can fast for between six and nine months, and their blubber, once thought to keep them warm, acts as a huge fuel tank. But if the journey takes two to three months, why should the krill still be there when they arrive? Fortunately, krill shoals can be huge; sometimes they cover an area the size of Scotland, so even latecomers are assured a meal when they finally turn up.

Opposite Pelicans migrate using the rising columns of hot air known as thermals. They find each invisible elevator by listening to the infrasound created by the moving vortex of air.

Left Seeing with sound. The ear of the long-eared bat picks up echoes from its own ultrasonic calls. By decoding these reflections it can create images in total darkness.

Ultrasound

Just as our limited hearing abilities prevent us from hearing infrasound, at the other end of the scale there are many sounds pitched too high for us to hear. These ultrasounds make up one of the most extensive sensory worlds denied to humans.

Our hearing fades out around 20,000 hertz, but an incredible variety of animals, ranging from insects to dolphins, make and hear sounds pitched far above this. Among mammals, size affects the ability to eavesdrop on this world. As a rule, the smaller the animal, the higher pitched the sounds it can hear. Almost all small mammals, including rodents such as mice, hamsters and gerbils, and insectivores such as shrews, hedgehogs and moles, use these high-pitched sounds.

Tickle a young rat on its stomach and it will giggle with sounds you cannot hear. This ultrasonic laughter is similar to the laughter of children, who also are more ticklish than their parents. The reason the young of both rats and humans laugh so much is thought to help separate the rough and tumble of play from more threatening, aggressive interactions. Although laughter may mean the same to both of us, because of our sensory differences it is impossible for us to share the joke. But we have more than laughter in common with rats. Male rats squeak rhythmically in ultrasound as they mate and later indulge in high-pitched post-coital singing.

Seeing with Echoes

Ultrasound has many uses, but it also has an important characteristic: it is reflected back by vegetation, which muffles the sound. Small rodents can therefore chatter in their runs without being overheard by predators. This special nature of ultrasound gives some animals even more incredible powers.

As small mammals career down their tunnels and runs they often squeak in ultrasound. At these frequencies, sound waves bounce off grass stems as though echoing from the walls of a tiny cathedral. Just as we can estimate distance by timing an echo's delay, small mammals can assess the proximity of an object in a similar way. Animals as varied as moles, shrews, hedgehogs and rats all use such basic echolocation. Creatures that live in total darkness have refined the system.

The Malaysian white-tailed shrew searches for cockroaches among the guano of bat-infested caves by squeaking and listening for echoes bouncing from its prey. The reflections give only limited information, but it is enough for the shrews to find a meal in total darkness. Above their heads are creatures that have taken this basic echolocation and perfected it to a point where they can create images from sound.

The screeches of insectivorous bats can reach an incredible frequency of 200,000 hertz. At these ultra-high frequencies, sound reflects from even the tiniest object. By analysing these echoes, bats construct a picture in sound. They can improve detail by pulsing their calls. Normally this happens 25 times each second, but they can increase the rate to 200 times per second for extra resolution. At these higher rates they can perceive a midge 20 metres away.

A bat's sonar is so powerful that it can identify size, weight, flight speed, direction and type of insect. The system may be based on sound, but the bat's brain processes the information as if it were dealing with images.

The highest sound frequencies give the best resolution, but these are readily absorbed by the atmosphere and penetrate only a short distance. To combat the problem bats sweep each sound pulse so that it rises in pitch like a siren, enabling it to include more penetrating low frequencies alongside the detail-resolving high frequencies. Some bats also use other techniques to improve resolution.

Most of us have experienced the rising pitch of a siren as a police car races towards us and the falling pitch as it races away. Some bats have ingeniously harnessed this effect, known as Doppler shift, to locate their prey. Instead of using short pulses they create longer bursts of ultrasound. As a moth approaches, the returning echoes appear to change pitch, giving precise information about relative speeds. Some species, such as long-eared bats, work like speed cops, lying in wait and scanning the air with their own ultrasonic speed-gun. When a victim comes into range, the bat uses Doppler shift to calculate distance and air speed before flying out and plucking its prey from the air.

Bird Sonar

Birds cannot hear ultrasound, but this has not stopped some of them developing an echolocation system – they just use lower frequencies. The cave-dwelling oil-birds of South America and the cave swiftlets of South-East Asia have independently evolved a sonar system that is audible to humans. Most of the oil-bird's echolocating clicks are around 2000 hertz. At these frequencies they can only sense objects larger than a football, but even so they can easily avoid bumping into the walls of the cave in which they live. The cave swiftlet's echolocation system works at slightly higher frequencies, allowing it to resolve objects as thin as a pencil.

Dolphin Sound Imaging

The toothed whales, such as dolphins and porpoises, are the masters of sound imaging. Their system is similar to that of bats, but dolphins create sound in their larynx and then focus it into a beam through the dome-shaped structure on their head, known as the melon. The returning echoes are picked up through the lower jaw.

Dolphins have amazing
SuperNatural powers.
But their legendary
ability to save human
lives is still unproven.

A cruising dolphin emits pulses ten to twenty times per second, but this rate rockets to 200 per second as it homes in on a fish. Instead of sweeping through a range of frequencies like a bat, it discharges an instantaneous sonic burst containing a wide range of frequencies; the highest of these can reach 200,000 hertz. It decodes the complex echoes to gather a detailed picture of the scene and improves definition by tuning the frequency band to match the object under investigation. By being so precise it can resolve wires as thin as a third of a millimetre.

Dolphins can alter the frequency of their ultrasonic beam and this appears to give them an extra power – they can turn it into a sonic weapon. They seem capable of tuning their high-intensity sounds to a frequency that causes the fish's swim bladder to resonate, and this is thought to cause their prey's body tissues to vibrate like jelly, fatally disorientating the unfortunate fish.

As well as finding and stunning fish, dolphins use echolocation to penetrate the gloom of the ocean, allowing them to follow undersea ridges and other physical features hundreds of metres away.

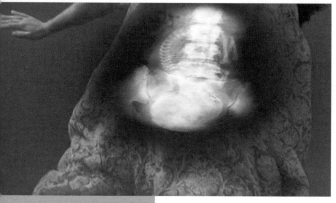

A dolphin's ability to 'scan' other life forms may be the reason it seems to find pregnant women particularly interesting.

Using echolocation gives dolphins surprising powers – other life appears like an X-ray. Body tissue is 90 per cent water, so the dolphin's scanning waves pass through it relatively unhindered – only the bones and air cavities reflect the sound. Fish appear as a ghostly outline with their skeletons and swim bladders shining conspicuously, and we too appear vaguely see-through – the dolphin not only sees our outline, it also observes a ghostly imprint of our skeleton and air-filled lungs. This view is similar to that of a hospital ultrasound scan and a dolphin inspecting a pregnant woman would 'see' the living foetus in a similar way.

In encounter groups where people meet dolphins, these cetaceans often show a special interest in pregnant woman. Whether this is because their echolocation allows them to discern the embryo or because of a chemical attraction is unknown. Whatever the reason, dolphins' interest in humans is part of a long line of anecdotal information that dates back centuries. Throughout history there have been many reports of dolphins rescuing drowning people and even chasing off sharks. Is there a scientific basis for this behaviour?

When a dolphin scans us in ultrasound it sees a creature that looks far more like another dolphin than a fish. We are of similar size and we share a skeleton, a mouth, throat, nasal passages and two air-filled sacs. Because of this similarity any curiosity or amicable behaviour directed towards us might simply be a case of mistaken identity. Dolphins support injured fellows at the surface to prevent drowning, so humans in trouble might elicit a similar response.

As dolphins are playful throughout life, it is equally possible that in their treatment of us they are simply playing with an interesting animal that has suddenly appeared in their world. In any case, dolphins are intensely social creatures and lone individuals are desperate for companionship, which may explain the many cases of single dolphins befriending humans. In some instances, sexually frustrated lone males may be seeing a human as a potential partner, so some of the behaviour interpreted as rescuing could simply be the result of an amorous approach.

Dolphins 'saving' people from the attacks of sharks is probably an extension of their natural response when faced with an aggressive predator. They react even more strongly when young are present and a helpless human may trigger a similar defensive reaction.

Whatever the reason, there appears to be something magical in the contact between humans and dolphins that simple, cold, scientific analysis devalues. What is truly awe-inspiring is the coming together of two intelligent creatures with two totally different sensory views of the world. Compared to our limited perspective, we are being contacted by animals who possess truly extrasensory powers.

There are many other SuperNatural powers of animals, some of which are so strange that they are often considered paranormal, as we shall see in the next chapter.

2

P A R A N O R M A L

What do we mean by the paranormal? In the past, so little was known about the world that any strange event which conflicted with the expected was filed away in the paranormal drawer. In the Middle Ages this drawer overflowed with mysteries. Much of the natural world was an enigma. Many of the fabled animals of the time were garbled descriptions of real animals: scaly dragons arose from accounts of Nile crocodiles, once kept by the Egyptians as sacred beasts; unicorns were derived from early reports of rhinoceroses, the supposed power of their ground-up horn still a potent belief today. Even less exotic animals were said to possess paranormal powers. Black cats were thought to be the familiars of witches and their reflective eyes, an adaptation for night vision, were interpreted as the flaming eyes of the devil.

Even today natural occurrences occasionally seem to touch the paranormal. Cats are sometimes born with wing-like extensions to their bodies, a mutation that in the past would have struck terror into any village. Rats may be found with their tails linked together, creating a wheel-like living creation *that was once known as a Rat King. We still find these phenomena strange but, as science can now proffer an explanation, we no longer regard them as paranormal. As knowledge increases, accurate revelations about the physical and sensory worlds of animals have shrunk the paranormal realm to a few intriguing anomalies.*

But not all the paranormal beliefs of former times were simply the result of lack of knowledge; some, like the vast folklore that grew up regarding witches' potions and herbal remedies, accurately identified the medicinal properties of many plants. Science for a while treated claims made for these plants with scepticism, but their value is now being recognized again and, what is more, as we discover more about the powers of animals we find that they value these plants, too. Nevertheless, among the many animal powers that we now understand, there are still some which seem so miraculous that, when we compare them with our own limited abilities, paranormal seems the best epithet to use.

Raining Fish

Reports of fish raining from the sky hover on the thin boundary between the unexplained and the limits of present knowledge. Such tales date back to the era of the Ancient Greeks, but the phenomenon is far from mythological – in this century there have been hundreds of well-documented reports; sixty have come from Australia alone, and Britain, India, the USA and parts of Africa have all experienced fishy downpours. The details vary. Sometimes the fish tumble while still alive, flapping helplessly on the ground as though just splashed out of some celestial lake; sometimes they plummet dead or frozen, as if discarded from an orbiting supermarket freezer. To add to the confusion they may descend in a mixture of the different states, and falls may involve anything from a single fish to cascading shoals of several hundred.

Such bizarre events attract equally strange explanations. The ancients believed they were witnessing spontaneous generation, whereby nature, which was assumed to abhor a vacuum, created life to colonize new bodies of water. An imaginative, but equally fanciful explanation suggested that fish were migrating using the power of teleportation, vanishing from one place to materialize in another. Although this has a contemporary sci-fi ring, the idea was actually proposed nearly a hundred years ago.

Today, there are more rational explanations for these strange deluges. Fish that fall singly or in small numbers are the easiest to understand – birds have probably dropped them. Fish-eating birds carry their catches in their crop or their talons and this makes them easy targets for scavengers, which dive down and harry them. In this aerial dogfight the victim will often shed its load to help its escape, giving the marauder an easy meal. Such confrontations are surprisingly common; several birds, including skuas and frigate birds, make a living from this kind of piracy. If they fail to catch the regurgitated fish it would appear to an observer that it must have fallen from the sky.

Tumbling shoals of fish are less easily explained, but the hidden power of the wind may provide the answer. Tornadoes are among the most studied of all weather phenomena, but their unpredictable nature has helped them remain an elusive and mysterious subject. However, studies using Doppler shift radar and analysis of the destructive wake these twisters leave behind have revealed a great deal about their enormous power.

Although tornadoes are relatively slow-moving, air within their core churns around at over 500 kilometres an hour. Tremendous drops in air pressure create such huge suction that natural laws appear to be turned upside down. Fragile wheat stems are converted into lethal darts capable of penetrating tree trunks as though fired by some cosmic blowgun. Wooden shards from buildings, sliced and shattered in the spinning vortex, become air-powered missiles that can pierce solid iron.

A tornado also has awesome lifting power – it can rip houses from their foundations and spin them like clothes in a drier; it can pluck up cars and trucks like toys and throw them angrily across the countryside. But it is a fickle wind. When enraged, it rips asunder anything it touches, but it also appears capable of tenderness. It can pluck a horse from a field, transport it 3 kilometres and set it down unharmed; like Dorothy in *The Wizard of Oz*, people have also survived similar unscheduled flights.

A wind capable of carrying people and livestock in its volatile embrace must also have the power to carry and disgorge fish. But if tornadoes are the answer to raining fish, why are they so rarely mentioned by observers?

Tornadoes are the kings of wind, but there are other lesser varieties, such as whirlwinds and dust devils, that can creep by unnoticed but still summon surprising lifting power. It may be that these smaller rotating winds have given rise to the phenomena known as corn circles. Circular impressions in the crop have been reported for hundreds of years and have recently been attributed to the landing marks of alien craft. Hoaxers have now admitted creating the more elaborate modern designs but the basic corn circle of legend is likely to be the work of wayward wind vortices.

When they pass over water, strong winds show another power – they suck the water up into a rotating aquatic column known as a waterspout. Any fish at the surface would be drawn upwards in this liquid conveyor until they reached the angry interior of a storm cloud. Buoyed up inside the tormented clouds they could be

transported huge distances. By the time the raging forces had calmed down, the fish would be disgorged far from their original homes. The fact that many fish falls feature frozen fish and are often accompanied by hail is consistent with a brief sojourn inside a storm cloud.

A wayward wind seems the most rational explanation for falling fish, but as with so many of these scientific explanations it does not fit the facts of every account. It also does not explain why fish falls usually involve a single species at a time.

Fish are not the only animals to fall from the sky. Salamanders, freshwater shrimps, snails and crayfish have all featured in mysterious raining incidents. Other favoured skydivers are froglets and toadlets, although their materialization in rainstorms may have a simpler explanation. Young frogs and toads migrate from their home ponds in heavy downpours and this mass exodus can suddenly transform the ground into a hopping swarm of tiny amphibians. It would be easy for any observer to assume that they arrived with the rain rather than appeared because of it.

The common expression 'It's raining cats and dogs' seems, on the face of it, to refer to showers of animals, but the expression has medieval origins and it is more likely to relate to the abysmal drainage of old city streets. At that time, a heavy downpour could flood many animal hideaways, drowning their inhabitants, especially pups and kittens, and washing them on to the roads.

Another strange fall from the sky is the luminous jelly that sometimes appears scattered over the countryside. It was first noticed on Welsh hillsides and given the name *Pwdre ser* or 'rot from the stars'. It was originally thought to have extraterrestrial origins, but a more down-to-earth explanation for its strange appearance involves predatory birds. When herons and other birds feed on frogs, early in the breeding season, the catches often contain a gelatinous mass of unlaid frog spawn. This swells on contact with water in the bird's stomach so, to avoid feeling bloated, the birds regurgitate the unpalatable jelly. As this gelatinous vomit absorbs water from the surrounding vegetation it becomes *Pwdre ser*.

Herbal Medicines

Showers of fish and other raining phenomena at first seemed to defy science and, until rational explanations were forthcoming, they were readily dismissed as fantasy. Another area that straddles the borderline between scientific knowledge and superstition is the 'medicine' of witch doctors and herbalists. New revelations from the animal world show how ancient their treatments might be.

Recently there has been a growing acceptance of the usefulness of herbal remedies. What was once considered cranky and unscientific is now becoming established as a complement to conventional medicines. It is surprising that a

Opposite An unusual sight – a huge waterspout accompanied by a bolt of lightning over part of Florida. Could this natural force be behind the mystery of raining fish?

schism between the two orthodoxies ever developed, as so much of conventional medicine derives from natural ingredients or synthesizes chemicals that mimic natural cures. Some 60 per cent of today's drugs are wholly or partly natural in origin. The miracle drug aspirin was originally produced from willow bark, while the anti-oestrogen tamoxifen, used in the treatment of breast cancer, is derived from the yew – a tree steeped in folkloric power.

Today tribal shamans, once dismissed as witch doctors, are consulted for their knowledge of healing plants, but, with so many cultures losing contact with their traditional ways, this valuable wisdom is vanishing fast. Such knowledge has an ancient history, but the extent of its antiquity is only just being revealed – we are discovering that our nearest living animal relatives also practise herbal medicine for a variety of common ailments.

If a chimpanzee is in pain or feels unwell it searches the rainforest for a cure, seeking the same leaves and herbs that are used as remedies by the local people. Like them it treats bacterial and fungal infections with leaves from the *Aspilia* plant and uses other plants to treat stomach upsets or rid the body of parasitic worms. Chimpanzees and the local people even use the same primitive herbal form of birth control, inducing abortions with *Combretum* and *Ziziphus* leaves. Chimps are believed to take the plant if their populations grow too high.

Other primates, including baboons, lemurs and vervet monkeys, also share many of the same medicines as East African tribes, using plants such as acacias, smilax and hibiscus to cure a range of ills. When baboons are suffering from diarrhoea they treat themselves with the leaves of the Sodom apple (*Solanum incanum*). When they are infected with *Shistosoma* worms, a harmful gut parasite, they destroy the infections with the fruit of the *Balanites* tree. Menstruating baboons even have a treatment for period pains, taking the leaves of the candelabra tree to ease their discomfort.

Other animals besides the higher primates can also cure themselves. Some, such as the African clawed toad and the yellow-bellied toad, are natural chemists, synthesizing their own medicines. Their skin secretes compounds that combat bacteria as effectively as penicillin. Because the toads often live in stagnant water, these medicinal compounds guard against skin infections. Honey-bees and the *Cecropia* moth produce similar antibiotic chemicals to fight their diseases.

When rabbits wash behind their ears they dose themselves with their own vitamin supplements. Oil on the ears contains a chemical that breaks down when exposed to sunlight to form vitamin D. The long ears act as sun traps, helping this chemical change to happen. The rabbits then transfer the vitamins to their mouths when they lick their paws.

As well as coping with illnesses, animals also need to combat the poisons that exist in their food. As we saw in Chapter 1, most plants protect themselves with tannins or alkaloids that can be dangerous if eaten in quantity. We use a simple neutralizing technique to tackle this problem – cooking. By boiling or baking vegetables such as potatoes and cabbages, we render their toxins harmless. We have also employed thousands of years of selective breeding to make many of our crops more palatable, but there is a downside – animals find these neutralized crops as irresistible as we do and become pests.

As unmodified plants protect themselves with poisons, stomach upsets are a hazard of daily life for wild animals – and they swallow many of the same cures as us.

Charcoal is a prescribed treatment for many cases of human food poisoning – eat the deathcap mushroom and it may be your only hope of a cure. This same antidote is also well known to the red colobus monkeys of Zanzibar. These monkeys live on the young, protein-rich leaves of mango and Indian almond, but the trees fight back by lacing them with unpalatable chemicals called phenols and other poisonous substances. To deal with these poisons the monkeys have learned to take a daily dose of charcoal in their diet.

Although charcoal is difficult to find in the wild, wood burning in the forest creates a ready supply of this valued antidote, which the monkeys either steal from charcoal burners or pluck from bicycles carrying the charcoal in baskets into town. Mother colobus monkeys teach their young the benefits of this remedy and, like female Fagins, they also school their young in the techniques of thieving from the charcoal burners.

Another human treatment for stomach upsets is the refined clay known as kaolin. South American macaws use natural versions of this simple cure to neutralize poisons in their diet. In the early morning hundreds of these colourful parrots descend on exposed riverbanks to dose themselves with clay before they start foraging. For the same reason, the local people regularly ingest clay with their meal. Potatoes are a mainstay of their diet but, as wild tubers have not been subjected to the thousands of years of selective breeding mentioned above, they still contain dangerous toxins. Eating them with clay neutralizes their harmful effects and helps guard against stomach upsets.

Even the domestic cat has its own gastric remedies. By eating grass, it cleanses poisons, fur balls or unwanted food from its gut. Lions and other big cats use the same basic treatment.

Besides natural medicines, animals have discovered natural insecticides, too. Many birds of prey, particularly eagles, bring aromatic leaves back to the nest. This green garland, once thought to be purely decorative, is now known to keep

parasitic insects at bay. Similarly, in southern Africa, buffalo often decorate their horns with the leaves of pungent plants, creating a verdant head-dress that acts as a fly deterrent. Recently, when there was an outbreak of malaria in Calcutta, India, house sparrows started to line their nests with the quinine-rich leaves of the krish-nachura tree (*Caesalpina pulcherrima*). Quinine is the natural cure for malaria and is responsible for the bitter taste of the old colonial favourite remedy, the gin and tonic. The birds also started eating the leaves, taking their anti-malarial medicine like the British Empire-builders of old.

Opposite Lemurs, like our nearest animal relatives chimpanzees, seem to share our knowledge of traditional herbal remedies. This female will search for the relevant leaves to treat various ailments.

Left Natural healers. These colourful South American macaws know instinctively to ingest clay to neutralize the harmful poisons in the food they eat. A similar technique is used by the local Indian population.

Anting

As well as protecting themselves from illness and insect attack, animals indulge in strange rites that help condition their coats or plumage. In one of the most baffling and bizarre examples of animal behaviour, some birds willingly subject themselves to the frenzied attacks of ants. The ritual varies from species to species, but the core of this seemingly masochistic rite involves a bird disturbing an ants' nest and provoking the occupants into a fury. Some birds, such as jays and red-tailed magpies, simply lie on the anthill, wings outstretched, and succumb to the onslaught, but most, including starlings, rooks and weavers, indulge in a more elaborate display. The bird becomes a contortionist, extending a fanned-out wing to the ground and twisting its tail. It then picks up an ant in its bill and, using a quivering motion, applies the protesting insect to the underside of the flight feathers of its outstretched wing. It also applies them to its head feathers and the underside of its tail. As the ants fight back they unleash a chemical weapon – a corrosive spray of formic acid.

At least 250 species of songbirds indulge in anting, so there must be good survival reasons why. The most likely explanation is that the formic acid acts as an insecticide, helping to destroy feather mites. Due to its corrosive nature, the acid might also kill fungi and bacteria. Certain essential oils contained in the secretions probably act as a conditioner as well, making the whole ritual the perfect cosmetic makeover.

Firebirds

Birds perform other strange and varied techniques to care for their plumage. In fact, one of them may have given rise to the legend of the phoenix.

It is a common misconception that animals are terrified of fire. In reality, most are indifferent to it and some even seek it out. Among the fire-lovers are starlings and crows, which can frequently be seen perched on chimneys, apparently enjoying the acrid vapours. Because they sometimes appear to bathe in the fumes, taking up the same contorted posture seen in anting birds, it seems that the smoke might literally fumigate their feathers. But for some, the fascination with fire goes further.

In the Middle Ages, members of the crow family, including rooks, crows, jackdaws and magpies, were known as firebirds due to a strange aspect of their behaviour. They would fly down to the smoking remains of cleaned-out hearth fires, and carry a glowing ember back to their nest. In the era of thatched roofs, which were favoured nesting sites, this penchant for fire often resulted in a dangerous inferno. Even today houses are still set alight by incendiary birds.

In captivity, crows frequently display pyromaniac tendencies and some even learn to strike matches. They react to the fire by proffering their breast to the flames or standing over them with outstretched wings. This posture mimics that of anting or smoke-bathing birds and bears a striking similarity to that of the mythical phoenix. Now a familiar image on trademarks and heraldic badges, the phoenix was an Arabian bird which, at the point of death, built its own funeral pyre out of spices. It then sat on the pyre singing a sweet song until the sun's rays ignited the nest and consumed the bird in flames. From the ashes a new phoenix was born. Fire-bathing birds might have given rise to this legend because, seemingly miraculously, they usually emerge unscathed from the experience. They protect their eyes from the flames by a nictitating (blinking) membrane that acts like a second eyelid, and their mouths are safeguarded by copious quantities of saliva. They also avoid burning their feathers by fanning their wings to keep them in motion.

Spontaneous Combustion

Some animals that play with fire go one step further. There have been many reports of humans bursting into flames, but the only natural equivalent are the plants, like *Cistus* and dittany, which create volatile oils (see page 108); these ignite spontaneously and set the plant on fire, freeing their seeds in the process. Among animals, there is none that actually creates flames, but there is a beetle that does something almost as extraordinary.

The bombardier beetle acquired its name because of its bizarre ability to create a controlled explosion by chemical combustion – it houses an explosive chemical weapon is its abdomen. The design consists of a double chamber of different chemicals; one chamber contains hydraquinine and hydrogen peroxide which, although inert on their own, are potentially explosive when combined with activating agents held in the second chamber. The two kinds of chemicals are kept apart until danger threatens; then the beetle opens a release valve and discharges the contents into a combustion chamber. The reaction that results is explosive. A boiling spray of noxious chemicals and gas is propelled through a nozzle at the tip of the beetle's abdomen. The nozzle has a directional tip so that the spray can be aimed into the face of any predator. When birds, reptiles or insect predators are hit by this corrosive bombardment they immediately drop the beetle, allowing it to escape.

The bombardier's double-chambered mechanism bears an uncanny resemblance to rocket technology and there are other parallels in its design. The beetle pulses its irritant spray at up to 735 times a second, a technique that regulates the explosion and prevents the animal from cooking itself. The jet engines of German V1 flying bombs, deployed to devastating effect during the Second World War, used the same pulsing mechanism, but at the meagre rate of just forty-two times per second.

Below The strangest defence system af all? This amazing picture of a Texas horned lizard freezes the action as it shoots blood from its eye portal.

Opposite A basilisk or Jesus Christ lizard. This strange creature really can perform a miracle. It can walk, or rather run, across the surface of water.

Walking on Water

Other animals perform miracles of a different kind. The basilisk was a mythical beast, half cockerel, half snake, reputed to kill anything it looked upon with a single glance. In Central America, a strange lizard with a cock-like comb on its head and a fearsome scaly appearance has been given the same name. It lacks the mythological basilisk's powers, but possesses another almost miraculous ability. Its alternative name, the Jesus Christ lizard, gives a clue to its real skills – it can walk on water. It performs this feat by rising up on its hind legs, then racing across the water surface.

The secret of the 'miracle' lies in the air-filled potholes created under each foot as the basilisk runs. Its toes are lined with a fringe of scales, which momentarily trap the air and prevent the animal from sinking. Instead of walking on water it actually walks on air. It simply has to move fast enough to avoid the air pocket collapsing before it takes the next step. As it races to stay on the surface it can reach speeds of 12 kilometres an hour and, by keeping up the momentum, it can cross a 40-metre pond without sinking.

Tears of Blood

Another human 'miracle' involves statues, often of the Madonna and child, that cry tears of blood. Amazingly, there is an animal that does the same.

In the southern deserts of North America, three different species of horned lizards have evolved a strange but impressive array of defences. Covered with

fearsome spines that would make them an unpleasant mouthful for any attacker, they appear well protected against predators. They are also masters of camouflage, blending artfully with the desert sand or rock. If this protection is not enough, they attempt to intimidate their attackers, inflating themselves into a formidable-looking adversary and hissing angrily as they jump forward. And if this bluff fails to impress, they fall back on the strangest defence of all — they weep tears of blood.

To perform this feat, the lizard increases the blood pressure in the sinuses of its eye sockets until the walls burst and blood erupts, squirting from the eyes with such force that it can jet out over a metre. The predator is usually so shocked by this gruesome display that it leaves the lizard alone.

This behaviour is so bizarre that reports of it were questioned by science for many years, but the horned lizard is not alone in using blood as a defensive weapon. This 'auto-haemorrhaging' (literally 'self-bleeding'), as it is called, is common in the insect world. Ladybirds, for example, ooze blood from their leg joints. The blood may clog the mouthparts of insect predators and may even be poisonous.

Severed Limbs

Besides shedding blood in various ways, some animals take one step closer to the paranormal and actually discard parts of their bodies.

A hackneyed but effective horror-movie device features a severed limb that continues to thresh about when detached from a human body. This grisly happening has its animal counterpart and is so common it has even been given a name — autonomy. Amazingly, there are many animals that sacrifice their limbs willingly; crabs give up legs, starfish lose arms and many lizards discard their tails. In true B-movie fashion the severed body part often continues to writhe and wriggle as though it had a life of its own.

This weird behaviour is a disturbing defence against predators. The predator seems to suffer the same shock reaction as the movie audience and, as it watches the squirming appendage, the rest of the animal makes its escape.

Lizards can perform this gruesome self-amputation because the vertebrae of their tails are designed with predetermined fracture points. The Pallas glass snake (actually a snake-like lizard) is a master of the art and its name reflects its built-in fragility. Already legless, the Pallas readily discards its tail as well whenever it meets a predator. The tail is like delicate glassware and spontaneously shatters into fragments, causing the lizard to lose up to two-thirds of its total length. Special muscles that continue to contract even when detached from the body allow each piece to writhe convincingly with a life of its own, apparently causing the predator great consternation.

After such self-amputation, the tail readily grows back, enable the lizard to perform the same trick again, though the restored appendage never matches the perfect grace and length of the original. But for the lizard this is a small price to pay for being alive, and the fact that the new tail is just as brittle shows how valuable this fragility is for the animal's survival.

The red-sided garter snake has an even grislier defence – it can sacrifice its liver. In spring, natural limestone pits in parts of Manitoba, Canada, are filled with thousands of snakes recently emerged from hibernation. Conspicuous and near helpless, they are an easy target for crows. But the birds, faced with such an abundance of food, can afford to be choosy – they soon learn to locate and pluck the liver from the living snake. Although the snake's long body gives little away, the crows, like skilled surgeons, learn through experience where the organ is found and become adept at removing it with one well-aimed stab. Remarkably, the snake can survive without this vital organ for long enough to regenerate a replacement.

In some lower animals, detached limbs may literally have a life of their own. If a starfish loses an arm it soon grows a substitute, but if the starfish is cut in two both halves may crawl away and grow into two new individuals. Some starfish need only a tiny portion of the central disc and a fragment of arm to regenerate themselves in this way.

Sponges are even more resilient. Although these creatures look like plants they are actually colonies of individual animal cells. They can regenerate themselves more effectively than any other animal. Even if they are squeezed through a sieve of silk gauze until they are just a mush of cells, they can still miraculously reorganize themselves into a new sponge.

Virgin Birth

Another 'miracle' that is regularly performed by some animals is the phenomenon of virgin birth, more scientifically termed parthenogenesis.

Sex is the driving force of genetic diversity and it is as popular in the natural world as it is among humans. The biological basis for its universal appeal is its value in allowing genes from different individuals to be recombined to form new animals. The variation found in these new individuals makes them different from their parents and helps the animals adapt, through the generations, to changes in the environment.

Despite these advantages of sexual reproduction, several insects, such as stick insects and aphids, practise parthenogenesis. The most familiar are the rose aphids known as greenfly. If you could speed up time and watch from the moment the first sap-sucking aphid landed on a rose bush in the spring, until the summer's end, you would witness its awesome potential for reproduction. Replicant aphids are

squeezed from the parent's rear like peas from a pod. From these clones new aphids soon appear and, like Russian dolls, each version has another identical one inside. As thousands of proboscises siphon off the plant's life blood, the invasion of cloned greenfly soon endangers its host. Despite attacks from a host of predators, includ- ing ladybirds, lacewing larvae and angry gardeners, the aphids' population is hardly dented, yet their main defence is simply their phenomenal rate of reproduction.

Aphids can reproduce this quickly because all the clones are females and each one is created without sex. Males appear on the reproduction line only in the autumn. Then, for the first time in the year, aphids indulge in real sex. After a mad flurry of sexual activity eggs are laid and in this form the aphids survive the winter. In the spring, they hatch out to begin a whole new cycle of asexual reproduction.

As well as rapid reproduction, virgin birth has another advantage — if a popula- tion is devastated by natural disasters such as flood or fire, only a single individual needs to survive to start the process of repopulation. However, there are dangers to the strategy, too — as each individual is a clone of its mother it is equally vulner- able to any change in the local environment.

Because of its disadvantages, parthenogenesis is rare among higher animals, but the whiptail lizards of North America and Mexico sometimes practise it. Some lizard colonies have no males whatsoever. The Chihuahuan spotted whiptail seems to be unique in this respect; in this ultimate sisterhood no males have ever been found.

The Third Eye

In Hindu belief each person has a third eye, concealed from normal view, which is a channel of great power. It is found in the middle of the forehead, just above the eyebrows and this area is accentuated by caste marks or, among married women, by red, yellow or white spots.

Remarkably, many animals exhibit a third eye and it is found in exactly the same spot as a caste mark on a devout Hindu. In the tuatara, a prehistoric relict reptile still living in New Zealand, the third eye can actually be seen between the two normal eyes. Known as the pineal organ, it has a lens-like skin covering and a retina-like back, but it cannot form a proper image. In fish, amphibians, reptiles and birds, the pineal organ is buried just beneath the skin and it is sensitive to changes in light levels. In mammals, including humans, it has lost this close connection with the outside world and has become a pea-like gland which is nestled in the mid-brain. But even though it is close to the brain, the pineal has no direct nervous connection with it; instead it receives messages from the eyes. It reacts to information about changing light levels by secreting melatonin, a hormone that controls the timings of many different functions in the body. Although it remains a somewhat mysterious organ, like the Hindu's third eye, the pineal organ has been shown to have great power and influence over our bodies. Not all eyes are so benign.

The Evil Eye

The expression 'If looks could kill' alludes to the ancient belief that some people, like the legendary basilisk, possessed the demonic power to kill with just one glance, and real animals occasionally seem to share this fabled ability. In South America the stare of the jaguar has been reported to cause monkeys to drop out of the trees and in India and Africa leopards sometimes affect the local monkeys in the same devastating way. The most rational explanation is that the victim has suffered a heart attack. Meeting the gaze of a predator is stressful for any animal and the shock could easily trigger cardiac arrest in susceptible creatures.

Usually, the reaction of prey to predator is more measured. If the predator is spotted early enough, the prey will signal their alarm, frisk away to a safe distance, then turn to face their adversary. Predators that have been discovered in this way rarely give chase, often feigning disinterest instead. But once a predator has stalked to within striking distance of its prey and has been seen, the reaction is often very different. The prey may freeze, hesitant to flee, almost as if caught in a trance. The predator may appear equally reluctant to give chase. In this stand-off, a move by either animal will precipitate a chase, so the animals' eyes stay locked together until one of them breaks the spell. Variations on this relationship between predator and prey have given rise to a phenomenon known as charming.

There are many reported stories of predators using bizarre and hypnotic behaviour to capture their prey. The most common examples involve foxes or stoats. In these tales the predator rolls on the ground, somersaults or even prances around on stiff legs. Its victims show a curious fascination for this weird pantomime and gather round to watch. When this unsuspecting audience is within range, the predator suddenly switches from entertainer to attacker.

Whether such behaviour is deliberate is difficult to decide but, because prey animals are fascinated by their predators, they are often drawn towards them. As a safeguard, the prey makes alarm calls and fixes the predator with its gaze to ensure that the hunter knows it has been seen. More elaborate versions of this reaction involve the prey mobbing the hunter; this seemingly suicidal taunting relies on the fact that predators have to hunt by surprise.

If a predator appears to lose interest, as when it indulges in play, the prey can be lured into a false sense of security that may prove fatal. When a cheetah catches a gazelle, the rest of the herd often forms a curious circle around the victim. The cheetah then sometimes makes a second kill by chasing the rubber-necking onlookers. It is not too hard to imagine that some predators learn to charm their prey into making these kinds of mistakes.

Several snakes, including the African tree snake and Ceylonese pit viper, appear to make hypnotic movements that have the effect of mesmerizing their prey – although most animals apparently under snake hypnosis are more likely to be under the influence of their venom, having already been bitten before a human observer arrived on the scene.

When an animal is actually captured, its reaction sometimes produces a different trance-like state that may have even closer links to the poorly understood phenomenon of hypnosis.

Reports that animals can be hypnotized have an ancient history. In one of the most renowned demonstrations, a seventeenth-century Austrian monk placed a domestic chicken upside down on the ground and drew a line in the dirt away from its beak. The bird fixated on the line and appeared hypnotized for several minutes. The same trick can be done with a variety of animals. Place the head of a pigeon under its wing and it will enter a similar strange stupor. Stroke a weasel gently from nose to forehead and it will go limp and motionless for a short time. It happens to reptiles, too. Alligator wrestlers frequently include hypnosis in an act that climaxes with the alligator upside down and totally immobilized. In fact the phenomenon is so widespread that it has been documented in animals as varied as insects, crustaceans, fish, amphibians, reptiles, birds and mammals.

The state, known as thanatosis, typically lasts a few minutes but has been known to continue for hours. During this time the animals appear totally unresponsive, their legs become rigid, their heart and breathing rates drop and they often close their eyes as though dead. The trance usually ends suddenly as the animal stands up and often flees.

Opposite Who is hypnotizing whom? The swaying movements of the snake charmer create the impression of hypnosis, but the snake is simply following the movements of a potential predator.

Although there are many ways to induce thanatosis, they share a common theme — they all involve restraining the animal in some way. The idea that people can be 'scared stiff' might be a clue to what is going on. When animals are attacked by predators, their first instinct is to try to escape, but once they are caught, struggling soon becomes futile — it simply results in the predator strengthening its grip. By becoming immobile the prey increases the chances that the predator may lose interest and release its hold. Being motionless also suppresses the predator's instinct to make a killing bite. Anyone who has watched a cat playing with a mouse can see how such a simple strategy increases the mouse's chances of survival. The cat's interest is governed by the actions of the mouse — when it moves, so does the cat, but if it stops, the cat stops too. The cat may bat the stilled mouse with its paw to provoke some reaction, or it may toss the mouse in the air, but it is usually reluctant to kill. In fact, if the mouse continues to show no sign of life, the cat may well become distracted, giving the mouse a chance to escape.

Above Stoats have been seen to 'charm' prey by dancing hypnotically in front of them. This behaviour may exploit the natural inquisitiveness of prey towards a predator.

Opposite above This wild dog has immobilized a wildebeest by grabbing it by the lip; the same behaviour is used on zebra and is believed to release natural opiates in the animal's brain.

Playing dead is also effective against predators, such as foxes, that often bury prey in food stores. Ducks have been seen escaping from these larders some time after they were placed there by a fox. Feigning death is even more effective against predators that refuse to eat dead prey — they may simply pass it by.

Remarkably, the ease at which domestic fowl feign death is subject to a daily body rhythm, occurring most readily at dusk when predators are active. Such is the survival value of entering a death trance that many animals, such as opossums, have made spectacular use of it.

Playing 'Possum

The opossums of North America have given rise to a popular phrase for playing dead. When threatened by a predator this small marsupial first tries bluff, hissing loudly and displaying all fifty of its imposing teeth. If this fails to impress it tries another tack — acting: it falls on its side and lies perfectly still, eyes half open with its mouth in a rictus grimace of death. As if this dramatic turn was not impressive enough, it also

defecates and emits a foul-smelling green gunge from its anal glands — an acting technique that adds to the impression that it is dead and rotting. All through the performance the opossum remains conscious, checking occasionally on how the act is going down with the audience. If necessary it will stay in the role for over an hour. Finally, when it has no gallery to play to, it raises its head slowly, checks that the predator is not waiting in the wings, then races away to safety.

Although opossums have acquired a reputation for their theatrical death displays, there are many other animals equally capable of Oscar-winning performances. The European grass snake and the American hog-nosed snake both go limp when attacked, lying belly up and lolling their tongues out through a gaping mouth in an impressive imitation of death. If placed the right way up they tend to spoil the performance by over-acting, rolling over again to demonstrate that they really are dead. As with the opossum, their star turn involves releasing a foul-smelling fluid.

The most impressive death mimic is the West Indian wood snake; this winds up into a tight coil and coats its scales with a fluid that stinks of decomposing flesh. To complete the illusion special

Below Playing 'possum. The opossum's death-feigning is a protective defence designed to confuse a predator. Many avoid prey that appear to be dead.

blood vessels in the eye burst to redden the eyes and cause blood to run from the gaping mouth. The Asian board snake displays an interesting variant. It becomes totally rigid and stick-like when caught.

Feigning death when attacked also happens in invertebrates such as spiders, stoneflies, stick insects, beetles, moths and mites. Strangely, the ability has been bred into one of our domestic animals – there is a breed of goat that keels over at the slightest fright. Its legs stiffen and it falls to the ground, legs in the air. A car backfiring, a passing motorbike, even a person wearing loud clothes is enough to provoke the drop-dead reaction. These fainting goats, which exhibit an extreme example of thanatosis, were created by selective breeding by early American farmers. Their inclination to pass out at the slightest provocation helped protect flocks of sheep against coyote attack. The goats acted as decoys, allowing the more valuable flock to escape. Nowadays their sacrificial role is no longer required, but they are still preserved as a rare breed by several groups of enthusiasts.

Although an animal's immobility is usually triggered by predator attack, there are other reasons why it happens. Cats, including lions and leopards, carry their young grasped by the scruff of the neck and while they are being transported the cubs become completely motionless. Their immobility helps the mother as she carries her kittens to a new safe place. The cats never grow out of this freezing behaviour, so even an uncontrollable hissing moggy can be instantly subdued by 'scruffing' it by the neck.

The reason this behaviour is still found in adult cats is probably connected with the dangers of courtship. For the male, mating can be a hazardous time; the queen is dominant and she often reacts violently to the tom's advances. By grabbing her by the neck, the male causes her to become as docile as a kitten for the period of mating. Unfortunately, as soon as he lets go, her acquiescence vanishes and the tom often ends up with a clip round the ear from the queen's outstretched claws.

Horses display an interesting variant on this kind of immobilizing behaviour. It is possible to subdue a wild horse by twisting a cord, known as a twitch, around its upper lip. Although the twitch is not painful, it makes the horse docile and acquiescent by promoting the release of endorphins, the brain's natural painkillers. Wild dogs in Africa have been known to use a similar technique to subdue zebra they have surrounded – one dog holds the zebra by the lip as the others make the kill.

Zombies

A more intense version of hypnosis is the creation of the Living Dead, a rite which also has its natural counterparts. In the Haitian religion of voodoo, a black magician called a boker is believed to have the sinister power to create zombies, or the Living Dead. The boker performs a ritual in which a person is killed and returned to life in a soulless body; he then uses these so-called zombies as slaves. Some people dismiss the powers of the boker as fiction, but others believe that various natural poisons are used to send humans into this vegetative state. The deadly potion is said to be a blend of the gland secretions from the bouga toad, the venom of millipedes and tarantulas, the skin of poisonous tree frogs and the lethal poison of the puffer fish. This potent concoction is thought to send people into a coma and, when they are finally revived, they are so brain damaged that their memory has gone, and with it the power of speech.

The process of zombification has grisly parallels in the animal world. The European parasitic fluke *Dicrocoelium* spends the early part of its life inside an ant and the later part in a sheep. To make this difficult journey possible the fluke, like a voodoo boker, hijacks the ant for its own ends. By burrowing into its host's nervous system it causes a change of behaviour, making the ant crawl to the top of grass stems to give up its life in the jaws of the nearest grazing sheep. In this way the fluke completes its life-cycle. The spiny-headed worm that parasitizes woodlice also zombifies its host, causing it to leave its hiding place and wander around aimlessly until it is eaten by the next host – a starling.

But the most bizarre zombification is initiated by the parasitic worm *Leucochloridium*, found throughout North America and Europe. This also changes the behaviour of its host snail so that the latter is active and conspicuous when birds are foraging but in addition it has an ingenious trick to ensure that the prospective new host – the bird – gets the message. The parasites ultimately invade the snail's eyestalks and, by sheer numbers and by assuming vivid hues, cause the eyestalks to flash green. This neon-like advertising sign has a single message to any passing bird – 'Eat me.'

Astrology

Of all paranormal phenomena, the most commonly practised in the modern world is astrology. Our fascination with the stars also has its counterparts in the animal world.

In industrialized countries few people have a chance to contemplate the heavens. Buildings block much of the view and a perpetual blaze of light overwhelms most of the visible stars. Even away from cities, the pervasive pollution from light-spill and haze masks the nightly spectacle. But, in remote regions of the world, it is still possible to share the experience of our ancestors when, each night, they slept under a dazzling star-spangled ceiling. These people grew up with a familiarity with every constellation and from this knowledge a belief in astrology grew.

Although science rejects most astrological claims, the sun and the moon, as we shall see in Chapters 3 and 4, produce rhythms that ebb and flow through almost

Opposite Lion cubs become motionless when grabbed by the scruff of the neck, an instinctive reaction which allows them to be carried easily. The same behaviour calms the ill-tempered adult lioness when mounted by the male.

every living thing, controlling much of their daily existence. Because planets and stars are so much more remote, their influence is more difficult to accept. But studies in France in the 1950s appeared to establish a connection between the rising of different planets and the birth times of people in various professions. Doctors, for example, tended to be born when Mars or Saturn had just risen, and soldiers and politicians when Jupiter was in the ascendant. Whether these intriguing results prove a real connection with the planets or reflect some wider cosmic rhythm is difficult to say, but it suggests that there may be much more to discover regarding the real influence of the heavenly bodies.

Today, through the glare of artificial lights that now veils the night sky, we hardly notice the stellar movements, but most animals still live in a world where the stars are an integral part of their nocturnal experience. They may not use them to predict the future, but they certainly use them to guide their lives.

Migrating birds rely on their knowledge of the constellations to help them maintain a course. This was discovered when birds were confined in a large cage in which their view was restricted to the night sky above. The birds continued to attempt to move in the normal direction of their migration, but only when they could see the star field above them. Experiments in a planetarium that moved the night sky artificially confirmed that many migrating birds followed the stars. Warblers and indigo buntings changed their favoured direction in sympathy with the new position.

Because the Earth's rotation causes the night sky to appear to move, the constellations change their position throughout the night, making it difficult for them to

Left A natural astrologer? The huge eyes of the bushbaby are perfect for stargazing. In fact, they use the stars to find their way around the African bush.

Opposite Star trails. This long-exposure photograph of the night sky shows the movement of stars across the sky as the Earth rotates.

be used for navigation. Human navigators avoid the problem by fixing on a star, known as the Pole star, at the centre of the celestial rotation. In the same way birds seem to orientate using constellations near the pole star, although remarkably, like seasoned astronomers, they also learn the movements of other constellations. Birds' ability to navigate by the stars becomes more accurate when the entire night sky is visible. They are not born with this knowledge and have to experience the rotation of the celestial map for many nights before they gain the necessary navigational skills to use the stars as a reliable compass guide.

It is not known how many animals use the stars, but even the compound eyes of crabs can discern the brightest stars and it seems that on moonless nights moths also use the stars to help them navigate in a straight line. Some frogs, such as the southern cricket frog, rely on celestial cues to guide them and it is thought that many mammals use them, too.

Bushbabies have incredible nocturnal vision – their eyeballs are so huge that they take up most of the head and their bulbous eyes, complete with a mirror-like retina, gather every ray of available light. To them, the constellations must seem like a blazing light show and minor stars, invisible to our eyes, must shine down like lasers. When male lesser bushbabies seek a mate, they use this stellar map, emblazoned across the sky, to help them in their searches.

Bushbabies feel comfortable only amid the security of a tree or dense vegetation, but when courtship is in the male's mind he has to leave this refuge and cross large expanses of open ground. To lessen the risks he adopts one of the most extraordinary methods of locomotion in the natural world – pogoing. Using only his back legs, he makes huge leaps into the air, recoiling, as he lands, like a bouncing rubber ball. As he ricochets across the ground he may clear 5 metres in a single bound. For potential predators such as owls or genet cats, this erratic, rubberized jumping makes the bushbaby nearly impossible to catch. Even so, he avoids dark nights and restricts his pogoing to periods when the moon is up or the stars are clearly visible. The males migrate over several nights and each time they bounce off in a westerly direction, using the stellar map as a guide.

Aliens

In Mali, in the Homburi Mountains not far from Timbuktu, bushbabies live alongside a tribe known as the Dogons. The astronomical knowledge of these people almost defies belief – they knew about the existence of the 'white dwarf' Sirius B long before it was discovered by modern astronomy; they even knew that its orbit lasted fifty years. They were also aware of the existence of Saturn's rings and the fact that Jupiter had orbiting moons. To discover this they would need the visual acuity of a bushbaby, but the Dogons' astonishing explanation is that their stellar knowledge was given to them by a strange race of scaly, fish-like aliens who came from a planet orbiting a tiny star next to Sirius B.

Science tends to scoff at the idea that aliens have visited Earth, but few scientists now believe that life is not present in other parts of the universe. It may even be responsible for life on Earth.

The most accepted explanation for the origins of life suggest that it arose when the early atmosphere, subjected to the bombardment of cosmic radiation and electric storms, created a primeval chemical soup of organic molecules. In time, these molecules formed more complex coalitions and, through competition, the whole evolutionary process began. At the turn of the century a possible alternative idea was proposed. This suggested that Earth might have been seeded by life from elsewhere in the universe. This so-called panspermia theory proposed that living spores, resistant to the harsh conditions of space, rained down on Earth.

Although this theory gained little support, we now know that many of Earth's organisms create spores that could survive a journey through space. Several moulds and bacteria are resistant to the extremes of ultraviolet radiation, intense vacuum and extreme cold found there. It has also been calculated that particles of their size, repelled by the Earth's magnetic field and hitching a ride on the solar wind, could reach Mars in just a few weeks. In four years they may even have reached the outer planets. We do not know whether a game of interplanetary ping-pong, with life shifting from one planet to another, has ever happened, but the Earth harbours life that is resilient enough to make the journey.

A more recent proposal suggested that life was continually being transported here from far beyond the solar system. For their interstellar transport system, the space travellers used the cosmic nomads we know as comets. Locked up in the ice of the comet's tail were viruses that periodically swept to Earth, creating outbreaks of disease. The old idea of comets as omens of doom suddenly seemed to be given a new justification.

The theory that a comet's tail acted as a breeding ground for viruses never gained many supporters, but recent analysis of the Hale-Bopp comet showed that its tail actually contained all the hydrocarbons and organic molecules necessary for the genesis of life. It now seems that billions of years ago comets seeded Earth with the precursors of life – in effect, we originated from stardust.

The cosmos influences us in ways that we are still striving to understand. Not least of the mysteries are the forces that control much of the life of the planet; these are the subject of Chapter 3.

3

HIDDEN FORCES

*O*ur ancestors regarded the disappearance of swallows in autumn as one of the most SuperNatural events in the natural world. They would have been even more impressed if they had known that swallows spent the winter in Africa and that, in spring, they returned to the same barn they left the previous year. At the time such journeys would have seemed impossible and the hidden forces that guide the birds on their miraculous journeys were completely unknown.

We now know that the world is awash with mysterious and invisible forces that react with various life forms and account for many of their amazing powers. But we are still trying to fathom the details. Some of these forces are cosmic in origin, zapping us from the depths of outer space; others are brewed up by the sun, bathing our bodies with invisible waves. The moon provides another hidden influence; its gravitational field passes unnoticed through our bodies, creating sympathetic rhythms in the oceans and in many of the Earth's organisms.

Our ancestors had no doubt about the moon's magical power and were sure that it affected fertility and sanity; only now are we beginning to understand the interaction of forces that might ultimately prove them right. People in the past also believed that there was a connection between certain ill winds and a feeling of malaise, and that animals could predict earthquakes. All these near SuperNatural beliefs were born out of observation, but science, which once ridiculed the suggestions, has begun to unravel some of the mysterious forces that might be involved.

The Earth's atmosphere is a boiling cauldron, cooking up a soup of electrical charges. These become visible for just an instant when lightning splashes towards the ground, but their influence on life, as they bubble away in far subtler ways, is usually more covert. The planet also creates its own local forces, some gravitational, others magnetic, which affect life on Earth just as mysteriously.

We have succeeded in taming many of these forces and use them to drive our technological world. Without them radios, televisions, microwave ovens and computers would simply not exist. But although we understand the physics behind them, their impact on the Earth's organisms is still being investigated. One of the most enigmatic of these influences is the Earth's magnetic field.

The Earth Magnet

The world is a giant magnet and, like a child's bar magnet, it has a north and a south pole. This is a godsend for human navigators because, following the laws of magnetic attraction, the magnetized needle of a compass always points to the Earth's magnetic north pole. Migrating animals need to be equally certain about their direction and to keep themselves on course, they too refer to the Earth's magnetic field as well. But, despite intense research over many decades, the kind of compass these navigators use has proved elusive. Only now are we beginning to uncover some of the mysteries involved.

The puzzle is compounded because several systems are used. The first features the same natural magnetized iron crystals, known as lodestone or magnetite, that early sailors used for their compass needles. Tiny crystals of these miniature magnets are manufactured by the animal and scattered through various tissues. They were first discovered in 1975 in bacteria living in sediment in Woodhole, Massachusetts. These micro-organisms are too small to be affected by the Earth's gravitational pull, so instead, for the two hours of their short existence, they use the magnetic crystals to guide them into the sediment. Since this discovery, magnetite crystal has been found in almost every variety of migrating animal, including bees, monarch butterflies, tuna, rodents and many birds.

Turtles use these in-built miniature compasses to chart the series of migrations that make up their itinerant lives. As hatchlings, they escape the numerous hazards of the breeding beaches and slip into the open sea, taking refuge in various circulatory current systems that act as huge rotating crèches. As the turtles grow, they move into coastal feeding areas, where they stay until they mature; then, when they are ready to lay their eggs, the adults return to the same home beaches they left as hatchlings.

To accomplish these annual homecomings, turtles travel immense distances. Green turtles journey 2400 kilometres from the coast of Brazil to the remote outpost of Ascension Island in the South Atlantic, while Kemp Ridley turtles, found throughout the Atlantic and Caribbean, converge on a single beach in Mexico. Exceptional feats of navigation are needed to locate these dots of land in a vast featureless ocean, but remarkably the turtles always seem to arrive by the most direct route.

For us to achieve such pinpoint accuracy we need two navigational reference points, which is why we divide the globe into intersecting lines of latitude and longitude. Turtles appear to rely on a similar grid system, but one based on two different components of the earth's magnetism. One reference detects the varying strength of the magnetic field across the globe; the second senses the angle at

Previous pages
In electric storms some of the most elemental forces of nature become visible. They, and other unseen forces, exert a hidden influence on many creatures' lives.

which the lines of magnetic force intersect the Earth. By combining this information the turtles create a grid map which tells them exactly where they are at any one time.

Magnetic Vision

Our vision depends on pigments in the cones and rods of our retina that become energized when light falls on them. Remarkably, some of the photo-pigments in a bird's eye appear also to be affected by magnetic fields. European robins, Australian silver-eyes, American bobolinks and pigeons have all been shown to have a magnetic sense that needs light to operate. So it is likely that most birds share this extraordinary way of detecting the Earth's magnetic field.

The magnetic information probably appears in the bird's vision as two bright or colour-coded spots indicating the position of the north and south poles. This compass system needs light of the correct colour to operate, and some birds, such as silver-eyes, become totally disorientated under red light.

Birds are believed to use the two systems in combination, the visual magnetic sense acting as a compass while the magnetite system gives information regarding position.

Newts have their own version of a visual magnetic sense to find their way back to their ponds. Their magnetic sensors are secreted in the 'third eye' known as the pineal (see Chapter 2). In newts one of the functions of the pineal seems to involve sensing four different compass points, which the newt probably perceives as four bright spots. Because the system is dependent on light it can easily become confused and the glow of artificial light may create a baffling red-light district for amorous newts, shifting their directional sense clockwise by 90 degrees and sending them away from their breeding ponds.

Electro-navigation

Sharks and rays use yet another way of navigating by the Earth's magnetic field.

As we saw in Chapter 1, sharks have the most sensitive electro-receptors in the animal kingdom, which they use to detect the body fields of their prey. It appears they can also use these sensors to detect the Earth's magnetic field, using the same principle as an electric dynamo. This is how it works. Dynamos create electricity when a coil or wire rotating in a magnetic field induces a current to flow. In the same way, the movement of the shark through the Earth's magnetic field induces a minute current in its electro-sensors. This dynamo effect allows the shark to detect the tiniest local variations in the Earth's magnetism. To improve its performance, the head of one species has become modified into a bizarre organ.

The hammerhead shark's strange head is thought to improve sensitivity to the Earth's magnetic fields by spreading its electro-receptors into a spaced array of sensors. The hammerheads appear to gather around areas of high magnetic intensity.

The hammerhead shark's extravagantly sculpted head puzzled scientists for a long time. The most convincing explanation for the design is that it acts as an enhanced magnetic sensor. By spreading the head out into a flattened hammer, the shark increases the distance between its electro-receptors, amplifying their sensitivity to any variations in the magnetic field. The shark's characteristic method of swimming, which involves yawing its head from side to side, could also serve to amplify any magnetic information. So if the hammerhead is so sensitive, what is it detecting?

The Earth's magnetic field is distorted by any local sources of magnetism. These variations are particularly intense anywhere that molten lava has seeped through cracks in the ocean floor. Here, high concentrations of magnetic material create mounds, ridges and valleys of magnetic force. These local variations of strength have no physical form, but if they were plotted as a map they would appear similar to the contours of altitude. Sharks seem to be able to read these subtle variations.

In the Sea of Cortez, near Mexico, spectacular shoals of scalloped hammerheads congregate around magnetic sea mounds, using them as a convenient daytime staging post. At night they venture out towards their feeding grounds in search of squid. As they travel they follow magnetic pathways which are outlined purely by steep variations in magnetic intensity.

Although they lack electro-receptors, ocean-going mammals, such as whales and dolphins, also appear sensitive to these invisible magnetic roadways. What happens when they lead the whales astray may explain one of the great mysteries of the animal kingdom.

Each year, in some unfathomable suicide pact, between one and two thousand whales take their own lives by throwing themselves on to the shore. The phenomenon occurs in only a handful of species, such as sperm, pilot, killer and some of the beaked whales. But all these species have one thing in common – they live in groups with strong social cohesion, so, if the leader beaches, the others tragically follow. Their strong bonds of friendship appear to override any individual's desire to save itself.

A combination of factors seems to result in these strange sacrifices and most explanations involve some kind of navigational accident. Coastal species, well acquainted with the local environment, are unlikely to get lost, so illness or a disorientating disease of the inner ear is the most likely explanation for their beachings. But ocean-going species, less familiar with the hazards of negotiating shallow waters, could easily make fatal navigational errors. Their sonar may become confused by the reflections given off by long, sloping beaches, but the fault may also lie with their magnetic navigation system.

Strandings often occur on beaches where magnetic roadways happen to run into the shore. Whales, like hammerheads, probably use these invisible magnetic lines to guide them through the featureless ocean. As they unwittingly follow these byways towards the shore, they may realize their error only when the water is too shallow to allow them to turn back.

Solar Storms

Another event that seems to precede some whale strandings happens 150 million kilometres away, in the body of the sun. It has equally catastrophic effects on human navigation.

The sun is in a constant state of magnetic flux, reaching a peak of activity every eleven years. When it is at its most active, sunspots blemish its surface and solar storms erupt far into space. Electrically charged particles, known as protons and electrons, are flung towards earth and, when these cosmic rays reach the magnetic field, they create a raging disturbance known as a geomagnetic storm.

The effects of such a storm may be dramatic. The cosmic rays create static charges that disrupt or even destroy satellites and, as the bombardment reaches the atmosphere, they also upset radio communications. They can even induce currents in powerlines, causing the electric grid to fail, or blast computer chips, crashing systems. They also cause compasses to deviate from normal, fooling human navigation systems. They bring equal chaos to animal migrants.

When electromagnetic storms rage, homing pigeons may fail to reach their lofts and flocks of migrant birds can become severely confused, flying out to sea. Under the ocean, whales also appear to become disoriented in a way that is not fully understood. It seems that they rely on daily rhythmic variations in the Earth's magnetic field to set their body clock and when magnetic storms interfere with this synchronizing pulse, whales may find it difficult to ascertain where they are, making stranding even more likely.

The Aurora

Usually magnetic storms are invisible, but occasionally they excite the atmosphere to create the most spectacular natural light show on Earth. The Aurora borealis and Aurora australis, commonly known as the northern and southern 'lights', are eerie displays created as charged particles from the sun spiral down into the magnetic field of the Earth and collide with atoms in the atmosphere. The bombardment throws off electrons that crash into gas particles, creating an astonishing technicolour spectacle of billowing curtains of light. The ghostly manifestation is most often seen in high northern or southern latitudes, where the magnetic field is strongest, but when solar flares erupt, geomagnetic storms shift the Aurora into more equatorial latitudes.

Above Solar storms cause havoc on earth, destroying communication satellites and disrupting the navigation system of birds.

Opposite Birds, such as these migrating greylag geese, can become confused at times of high solar activity. Their magnetic sense can become disrupted and can lead them astray.

The same high-energy particles, cast off by the sun in a solar storm, dance inside each air molecule. Positively charged protons shelter at their core; surrounding them, like planets in a solar system, are negatively charged electrons. The two charges cancel each other out, but sometimes the electron becomes detached, leaving the molecule with a positive charge. If this electron then joins another molecule, it gives it a negative charge. These two types of unbalanced molecule, both positive and negative, are called ions. They are found in minute concentrations in the air, yet they influence life in a way we do not fully understand.

Normal air has slightly more positive ions than negative, but when their relative concentrations change they seem to have a noticeable effect on many creatures' well-being. Somewhat confusingly, positive ions generally have a negative effect on health, while negative ions have a positive influence. People exposed to negative ions seem to improve both in health and in athletic performance, while patients suffering from seasonal depression gain similar positive benefits.

Although ions in the upper atmosphere are formed by cosmic bombardment, those in the lower atmosphere are created as various types of friction shear off electrons from the air molecules. The most common cause is wind. Dry winds, such as the Mistral in France, the Fohn in Central Europe, the Santa Ana in California and the Chinook in Canada, all create a swarm of positive ions and, when these ill winds blow, a general malaise seems to affect much of the population. Moving water creates the opposite effect by absorbing positive ions and preserving negative ones, so waterfalls and beaches with rolling surf are rich in negative ions – which partly explains why these are such refreshing holiday locations.

The effect of these ions on the body is poorly understood, but positive ions appear to depress the rate that the tiny whip-like hairs, known as cilia, remove impurities from our lungs. They also seem to lower breathing rates, reduce blood supply to the trachea (windpipe) and modify the release of serotonin, the hormone responsible for our sleep cycle. High levels of positive ions increase serotonin concentrations, making us feel drowsy and depressed.

Because ions are sticky they attach to particles in the air, causing dust and pollen to tumble to the ground, making it easier for allergy sufferers to breathe. Negative ions also glue themselves to airborne bacteria, effectively 'washing' them out of the air and they must clean the air of airborne viruses too. Mice reared in ion-depleted air are more susceptible to viral infections such as influenza, and when ion levels are low we are probably affected in the same way, too.

In polluted air, a surfeit of particles can strip the air of all its ions, creating this harmful condition. Plants such as barley, oats and cucumbers grow better in air supercharged with either positive or negative ions, but they quickly languish in depleted air. Some of the ills of urban living may be due to this insidious tampering with the air's natural ion balance.

We notice the effect of these ions only indirectly, but it is possible that snakes have developed a way of sensing them in the air. Shuffle across an office carpet on a dry day and you soon become charged with static electricity, a fact that becomes shockingly clear the moment you touch a filing cabinet – an arcing static discharge is the result. In nature animals rarely build up these static charges, as their fur, feathers or bristles act as electrical discharge points. But, because their skin is dry and insulated, reptiles are different. As snakes slither across the ground they may acquire an electrostatic charge of up to 1000 volts, simply by friction. They may put this charge to good sensory use.

The snake's forked tongue, a symbol of duplicity and deceit, was once thought capable of stinging. In reality, this harmless sensory organ samples the air and carries scent particles back to a tasting organ in the mouth. Its two-pronged design

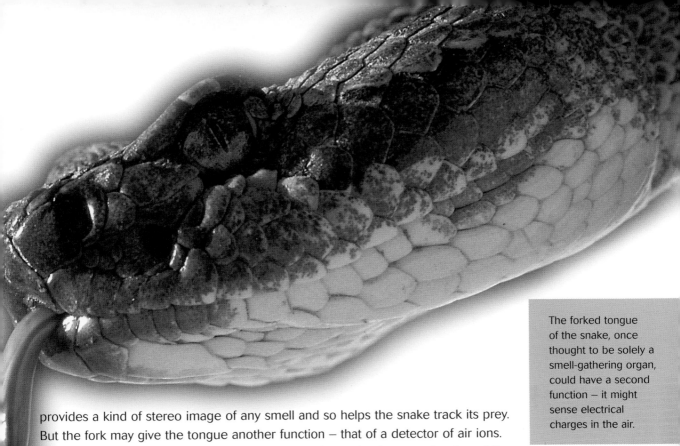

provides a kind of stereo image of any smell and so helps the snake track its prey. But the fork may give the tongue another function – that of a detector of air ions.

As positive electrostatic charges build up on the snake the scanning tips of the tongue are attracted by any negative charges in the air. (A similar effect is seen when a recently used comb, charged up with static, causes hair to be attracted towards it.) Positive air ions cause the tips of the tongue to be repelled. Snakes may use this information to detect air ion concentrations arising from plumes of moist air, either from the breath of their prey or from environmental features such as vegetation or holes in the ground.

If the theory is correct, the rattlesnake's rattle may have more than one use. The snake shakes its rattle as a warning when confronted by large mammals such as bison or people. It also seems to act as a static charge generator, creating positive electrostatic charges. This might be a refinement to a system that, in other snakes, relies on friction with the ground.

Electric Fields

Over this century we have added to the natural electrical cacophony with inventions that generate high-intensity electromagnetic fields, and these have an interesting effect on the animals that encounter them. If a creature passes close to any electrical equipment, a small electric field is induced into its body. In experiments, mice and rats have been shown to avoid high-voltage fields, and hamsters nesting near a high-voltage source will decamp and move their broods. The most conspicuous sources of electricity in the countryside are high-voltage power lines and these seem to create an invisible force field under which few birds will fly. Although birds do collide with

the lower voltage lines, accidents tend to happen on high-intensity lines only when the power is turned off for maintenance.

Bees are highly sensitive to electrical charges. A bee's whole body is negatively charged. This fact has been exploited by flowers, whose positively charged pollen is able to leap on to any visiting bee thanks to the forces of opposites attracting. If beehives are placed under power lines, the inhabitants soon swarm and leave; those that stay produce fewer brood cells and in the winter more bees die. In fact, bees seem to hate all electromagnetic fields and will vent their anger on any electrical equipment. But such loathing is far from universal; at least one species of ant reacts to electricity in a more positive way.

In the 1930s, a stowaway party of South American fire ants docked in an Alabama port and around ten mated queens disembarked. As each queen can create a colony of up to 300,000 workers, this founding party became an invasion force that soon overran the southern states. Although tiny, the ants are ferocious killers, viciously attacking their prey with venomous stings. Young birds, reptiles, rodents and even fawns have all succumbed to their frenzied attacks. On people a single sting is unpleasant, but in just six seconds hundreds of ants can cover a leg and, when they attack, they sting in unison. The result is the agonizing burning sensation that gave the fire ant its name. These attacks intensified as the ants found a home among human habitation. It was here that they discovered a strange predilection for electrical equipment.

In their quest for electricity the ants soon invaded air-conditioners, telephone systems and the ducts of electrical wiring. They swarmed over bare wires, contact points, fuses and switches, causing equipment to fail and, by chewing through power cables, frequently starting fires. On the roads they wreaked havoc by taking over the control boxes of traffic lights and they also interfered with the electrics of cars. At airports they created even more danger by tampering with landing lights. Why they should be so enamoured by electricity no one knows, but through their electrical tinkering these tiny ants have become the ultimate ghosts in the machine. Computers have now given them a new place to create devastation. Almost impossible to control, they continue to wreak havoc across the southern states of America.

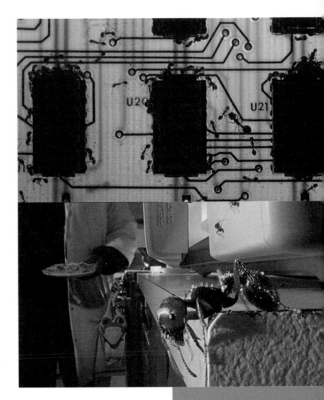

Above Electricity is an irresistible attraction to South American fire ants. They cause havoc by invading ducts and wiring, and, seemingly indestructible, can withstand being 'cooked' in a microwave oven.

Opposite High-voltage electricity pylons seem to create an invisible force field, and birds avoid flying under or perching on them. Plants, however, like pylons and appear to grow better underneath them.

The ants have another surprising quirk — they can be cooked in a microwave oven without coming to harm. Their invincibility is partly due to their size. The microwaves in the oven have a wavelength of about 13 centimetres. These flow round the tiny ant just as water ripples flow around a stem and then re-form. Another reason is the ants' frenzied activity — because the microwaves are far from uniform, the ants seem to be able to dodge any pockets of heat before these build up.

Normally, we become aware of natural sources of electricity only when storms build and lightning zigzags to the ground. The unleashing of these powers has always been associated with the supernatural. It seems that they do have a hidden influence on many forms of life.

Lightning occurs when charges of static electricity build up in a thundercloud. The base of the thunderhead becomes negatively charged and, as the cloud rolls across the sky, the ground below becomes positive. The charges are held apart as in a huge capacitor until a sudden discharge ionizes the surrounding air and becomes visible as lightning. Although we see a single flash, a pilot discharge acts as a path-finder for up to forty others, all crackling to the ground within a quarter of a second.

There is mounting evidence that plants can detect the growing electrical activity in a storm and react by shifting their metabolism into a higher gear. After a thunder-storm our lawns and shrubs look lush and green, presenting a very different appearance from when they have just been dowsed with water from a garden sprinkler. This suggests that the storm is creating electrical alchemy within the plant's chemistry. The secret probably lies with charged ions of calcium that act as messengers, switching on the enzymes that control growth.

Weather Prophets

Plants and animals are so sensitive to changes in the weather that, before computerized forecasts became available, their behaviour was, for many people, the only guide to what lay ahead. Whether it was cows lying down before a storm or high-flying swallows signalling good weather ahead, a vast folklore grew up to interpret the behaviour of nature's meteorologists. In Provence, farmers kept frogs in glass bell-jars so that their croaking would warn of rain and, across Europe, people watched the activity of plants to gain clues to changes in the weather. The scarlet pimpernel was even known as the poor man's weather-glass for its skill at predicting rainfall. Like marigolds, bindweed and corn sowthistles, it keeps its petals closed if a downpour is imminent. Other plants, such as wood sorrel and clover, react by closing their leaves. Some plants have more complex weather responses: if the flowers of the Siberian sowthistle shut at night it means the following day will be fine; if they open, showers are on their way.

These 'weather plants' are believed to be sensitive to a combination of temperature, humidity and light but, as we come to understand more about the electrical sensitivity of plants, it seems that a response to electrical charges in the air may also be involved.

Many animals also need to be meteorologists. In New Zealand the caterpillars of the porina moth live a subterranean existence, coming out only at night to cut grass and drag the stems down into their silken burrow. The brief lives of the adults coincide with a period of warm, rainy, misty weather; the moths then indulge in nuptial flights in the sultry night air, mate, lay their eggs and die. It is not clear how they know when to emerge – they may sense the falling barometric pressure that means a low-pressure front is approaching, or they may detect changes to the balance of air ions.

In contrast, the bogong moths of Australia live many months as adults. But because they face extreme seasonal weather changes they too have to become accomplished meteorologists. To avoid the blistering heat of the lowlands, where they spent their lives as caterpillars, they travel hundreds of kilometres to a cool refuge in the Australian Alps. Here, millions of these long-distance travellers spend the summer, clustered in the crevices and caves of granite outcrops, emerging only in the evening to indulge in a mass swirling flight. To reach their alpine retreat they need to predict the arrival of cold fronts that move in a southeasterly direction and will carry them towards their summer resting grounds. Like the porina moth, they may detect barometric pressure changes or air ions to make their unerring predictions, but the truth is that no one really knows.

Although it has been difficult to determine whether insects have a barometric sense, some animals certainly appear to monitor the weather in this way.

Bats that live in caves have a problem. Resting in conditions of constant temperature and humidity, they have no obvious way of knowing what the weather is like outside. Their secret skill lies in detecting changes of air pressure, using a built-in barometer, known as a vitali organ, in their middle ear. As well as knowing whether they should emerge at all, the eastern pipistrelles of North America appear to be able to predict the behaviour of the moths they prey on. By monitoring barometric pressure, they seem to know when moths are flying and even at what height they might be found. This barometric sense has another function; the bat knows exactly how high it is off the ground at any time.

A similar barometric sense is found in the ears of birds. If we had the sensitivity of a pigeon or a duck we would know which floor of a building we were on simply by detecting the change in air pressure. Migrant birds are so sensitive to tiny shifts in altitude that, even when clouds obscure their view of the ground, they fly within a narrow air corridor 20 metres high. As well as being useful as an altimeter, a bird's pressure sense helps it forecast the weather.

Rapid drops in atmospheric pressure precede most winter storms and, by detecting this dip, birds can prepare for the onslaught ahead. American goldfinches and black-capped chickadees react by going on a feeding spree, stoking up their internal energy stores to brave the bad spell.

For migrants, a wrong forecast can prove fatal. In spring, birds in the northern hemisphere set off only when temperatures are rising, pressure is falling and a south wind is blowing. In autumn, the opposite conditions provide the cue. In both seasons they seem to know in advance when the weather is changing in their favour.

Some birds show more complex migration patterns and use their meteorological skills to plot a course that makes the most of favourable winds. Blackpoll warblers make a 4000-kilometre migration that takes them from the eastern coast of North America to South America. Initially, they rely on a southeasterly wind that carries them in a seemingly dangerous direction out over the open ocean of the Bermuda Triangle. They are saved by the trade winds, which bring them back on course over the Caribbean and on to South America. Helped by these favourable

Opposite The orange ladybird is a long-range meteorologist, confounding experts by accurately predicting the severity of the winter ahead.

Below The mallee fowl or incubator bird is a living thermometer. It uses its bill to check the temperature of the mound of rotting vegetation in which it incubates its eggs.

air currents, blackpolls make the journey with a non-stop flying time of between 86 and 90 hours.

In Australia, birds can detect the weather changes that bring life to the parched desert interior. Here, droughts may last several years and when the rain finally arrives it makes a spectacular and torrential appearance. Dried out gullies become raging rivers, and lakes submerge the low-lying saltpans. With the deluge comes life. Midges, water fleas, water bugs and fairy shrimps hatch from eggs overnight to create a rich, animated soup of freshwater creatures. Frogs emerge from cocoons to feed on the bounty and then lay their eggs in the freshly made pools. Almost miraculously, birds seem to know that this harvest has arrived. Dabbling ducks, which need shallow water, are the first to arrive; diving ducks, black swans and herons soon follow. Many will have travelled hundreds of kilometres to reach these ephemeral lakes and rivers. How the birds know of the existence of these water sources is a mystery, but their ability to measure changing atmospheric pressure may provide an answer.

They may also be responding to deep infrasound (see Chapter 1). Bad weather sends an infrasonic warning ahead of it, enabling all animals that can hear these sounds to become meteorologists. The rumble of thunder is the high-frequency part of the sound, but there are infrasonic rumbles that travel even further. Air turbulence, stirred up by rain clouds, also creates infrasound. Such sounds could act as additional cues for avian weather prophets.

Australia is home to a particularly unusual weather bird — one with a thermometer in its bill. Instead of sitting on a nest like most birds, the mallee fowl builds itself an incubator. It first digs a huge hole, about 5 metres wide by 1 metre deep, which it fills with rotting vegetation and covers with sand. Then, over a period of several months, the female lays a succession of eggs in the decaying leaf litter in the centre. The heat of decay incubates the eggs but, to regulate their temperature, the bird continually adjusts the amount of vegetation covering them. The bill appears to act as a thermometer and, by probing it in the mound, the bird continually checks the temperature. Through this accurate monitoring, she keeps the eggs to within a degree of 34°C. The mallee fowl also appears capable of predicting the weather, making alterations to the mound hours before the weather change is about to occur.

Ladybird Fortune-tellers

Although we know some of the methods animals may use to predict the weather, there are many secrets remaining. Some of the most intriguing involve long-term forecasts. Animals that seem to know what the future seasons will bring possess powers that modern-day meteorologists would envy. One of the most studied of these clairvoyants is the ladybird.

Like other British ladybirds, the orange ladybird overwinters as an adult, hundreds clustering together in the same protective nook. These winter retreats are chosen in early autumn. The most sheltered sites are among leaf litter, but here the ladybirds have a high risk of fungal infection, so they choose these spots only if the coming winter is likely to be harsh. When mild winters are on the way they opt for healthier but more exposed locations. They are so accurate at determining the forthcoming winter that, over the ten years during which they have been studied, they have never been wrong.

It almost defies current scientific thinking that a ladybird could have knowledge of something as chaotic and unpredictable as future weather systems, but the reality of their behaviour flies in the face of such scepticism. Our ancestors would have had no problem in believing the ladybird's powers: they accepted that fruit trees, for instance, would produce a bumper harvest before a harsh winter as an insurance against possible destruction. They had equally strong beliefs about the influence of the moon on their crops. These beliefs, also treated by the scientific community with scepticism, now seem to have a basis in fact.

Moon Power

The ancients had no reservations about the moon's powers – temples were built to monitor its varying orbits and cycles and it was believed to control the fertility of just about every form of life. It was also strongly connected with madness – the Latin word for moon, *luna*, gave rise to the words 'lunacy' and 'lunatic'. The moon was also believed to influence the growing of plants and trees, and crops were planted with due deference to its phases. We are still trying to unravel the truth behind these ancient beliefs.

The moon is surprisingly small, its whole surface area no bigger than Africa. But, compared to the sun, it is relatively close to Earth and so its influence is out of proportion to its size. It is really a satellite, held in orbit by Earth's gravitational attraction, and in turn its own gravity pulls at the Earth. The most obvious result of this gravitational tug-of-war is the rhythm of the tides.

As the moon's gravity tugs at the Earth it creates two bulges in the oceans, one on the side nearer the moon and the other on the opposite side. As the Earth rotates, these two bulges travel across the globe, creating the twice-daily cycle of the tides. The creatures most affected by this tidal rhythm are those living at the interface between sea and land. This intertidal zone is alternately exposed to the searing heat of the sun or inundated by the pounding of the waves. To survive here the creatures must predict the violent changes.

In seafood restaurants, animals kept in holding tanks keep to the same activity cycle of their tidal home, even when displaced by hundred of kilometres. Reacting as if they were still safely tucked in the sand, live oysters gape at diners when their home tide comes in and clamp their shells shut, to avoid desiccation, when it goes out. Razor shells squirt at unwary waiters precisely at the time their home tide retreats, showing behaviour that normally propels them back into the sand before them become exposed to the air. When a scallop's home tide reaches maximum depth it claps its shells together and, with others of its kind, dances a water ballet that, in nature, would help them disperse in tidal currents. Lobsters and crabs, trapped in the same restaurant, also vainly hang on to the tidal activity rhythms of a home that they will never see again.

The secret of the shellfish's time-keeping is an internal clock synchronized to the tidal cycle. Most intertidal animals, such as shrimps and crabs, also have a second body clock that beats to a daily rhythm and a third kind that keeps track of another tidal cycle – the pattern of spring and neap tides.

Although the sun's gravitational pull is 26 million times stronger than that of the moon, its huge distance from Earth dilutes its pulling power to less than half the lunar strength. But by interacting with the moon's gravitational pull it creates the twice-monthly variations in tidal reach. At full and new moon, the sun and moon align together with the Earth, summing their gravitational pulls to create the high spring tides. In the moon's first and third quarters, the sun and moon are least in line and weak neap tides are the result. Many animals time their lives to these monthly or twice-monthly tidal cycles.

Throughout the summer months, on the beaches of California, small silvery fish known as grunions periodically strand themselves on the beach in behaviour that looks like mass suicide. At first, a single fish rides in on a wave, but gradually the numbers increase until the beach is a writhing mass of glistening bodies. These 'fish out of water' beach themselves for a good reason – to lay their eggs.

Each female that rides the waves to the shore may be accompanied by up to eight surfing males. If these surfers meet her expectation, she strands herself as high up the beach as possible, taking the males with her. As they flap around her, she arches her body, wriggles her tail and drills her rear end into the sand. While she lays her eggs, the nearest male embraces her and releases fertilizing milt. The next wave disturbs the entwined couple and washes them back into the ocean, at the same time burying the eggs under about 30 centimetres of sand. Protected by this wet blanket, the eggs develop until the hatchlings are freed on the next spring tide. The event is co-ordinated by the tidal cycle, taking place for three or four nights after the high tides associated with the full or new moon.

Opposite Crabs, like all marine creatures living on the shoreline, are affected by the ebb and flow of the tide. Their internal body clocks time this twice-daily cycle as well as the twice-monthly rhythm of the spring and neap tides.

Many other marine organisms show similar synchronized sex. One of the most famous is the palalo worm of Samoa and Fiji, which swarms on the neap tides of the last-quarter moon in October and November. For most of their life, these tropical relatives of the lugworm live in crevices in the coral but, when they sense the lunar beckoning, the rear ends of the worms break off and wiggle their way into the open sea. Soon the ocean is alive with wriggling detached bodies. Then something strange happens – their bodies explode, releasing eggs and sperm into the water. By spawning *en masse* the worms guarantee fertilization, and by sheer weight of numbers they soon satiate any predators.

A writhing mass of Californian grunion strand themselves in a mating ritual governed by the cycle of the tides. In the midst of this tangle of competing males, a female lays her eggs in the sand.

The moon's influence on sexual activity is most obvious in the oceans but, as the ancients believed, it can affect land creatures in similar ways. While marine animals seem to sense the moon's influence through changes in water pressure, for non-marine creatures the varying light of the moon is more important. Even though this is 300,000 times dimmer than the light of the sun, they use this cue to time their lives.

In Lake Victoria in East Africa, mayflies swarm two days after the light of the full moon has beckoned them to hatch, flying over the water in huge, billowing black clouds. The moon and reproduction seem to be synchronized in many animals, but the most interesting examples from a human point of view are found among our nearest relatives, the primates.

In Madagascar, lemurs go on heat just before full moon and their peak of sexual activity immediately follows; in Africa, guenon monkeys time their ovulation to coincide with the full moon. In the human world many ancient fertility rites were geared to the moon's phases, so is there any connection between the moon and our own sexual lives? One of the most intriguing hints that there may be concerns the length of the female menstrual cycle. On average it corresponds exactly with the moon's 29.5-day cycle, and nine such cycles make up the average pregnancy. Although some studies have discovered a link with the moon's phases and times of birth, the research is far from consistent. It is also self-evident that women's periods are far from synchronized. But the clue to what might be happening may lie in how lemurs regulate their cycles. If they are exposed to artificial illumination instead of naturally varying moonlight, their sexual cycles become unsynchronized, just like the menstrual cycles of their human relatives.

We now live in an environment where artificial light swamps the light of the moon but, in the past, it may have had a more direct effect on our fertility. When a group of women were experimentally given artificial illumination for three consecutive nights in the middle of their cycle, their periods soon became synchronized to the artificial lunar rhythm. There have been many other experiments that seem to confirm other aspects of these old beliefs.

One of the most bizarre convictions was the idea that people bled more around the time of the full moon, a fact confirmed, but not explained, by a study of tonsillectomy operations. There is similar tantalizing evidence for links between mental instability and the full moon. Two hundred years ago a plea that the moon had triggered a bout of madness could be used as mitigation in court and the anecdotal evidence of the behaviour of inmates at old 'lunatic' asylums bore out these claims. More recently, in America, several studies of murder rates confirmed a link with the moon cycle and another study of suicide rates found peaks corresponding to both the full and the new moon.

Harvest Moon

In classical times, the moon was also thought to influence plant growth – the phrase 'a harvest moon' confirms the universality of this belief. Pliny, writing in the first century AD, advised Roman farmers to pick fruit for market before the full moon, when the crops would be at their fullest. Medicinal plants were always gathered around the full moon and there was also a belief that this was a good time for planting crops. English folklore even attempted a scientific explanation, suggesting that the full moon brought more water to the plant. Modern science has been deeply sceptical about the link between plants and the moon, but a succession of experiments now suggests that the ancients were largely right.

The first experiments began in the 1950s when a scientist monitored the amount of oxygen used by a potato and discovered a rhythm of activity tuned to

Overleaf Earthquakes and volcanoes send out a barrage of warning signals, from infrasound and tiny tremors to eerie earthlights, which many animals seem able to detect.

the moon's daily cycle. Amazingly, the potato seemed 'aware' of when the moon rose and when it set. Carrots were then discovered to be equally sensitive. The moon's influence was found to affect more than vegetables when it was discovered that the changing electrical potentials of a maple tree also followed a lunar cycle. Then, in the 1970s, herbaceous plants in the Botanical Gardens of Padua in Italy were found to grow best around the time of the full moon. In another experiment, plants were shown to absorb different minerals more readily at the full moon and new moon.

As so often happens when science does not understand the mechanism behind a discovery, these experiments were not universally accepted. It was puzzling that the rhythms continued, even if the plants were shielded from the effects of moonlight or the moon's changing influence on atmospheric pressure. But recent experiments confirm that the moon really does have a profound influence on plants. Tree stems have been shown to bulge and contract following the daily lunar cycle, just like the tides in the oceans – and, like them, they have two 'high tides' a day.

The obvious explanation is that the moon's gravity must pull on the water, as it does in the oceans, but this is where scientific credibility becomes stretched. Ocean tides are noticeable because of the sheer volume of water involved, but in a tree the effect is too small to measure. The intriguing answer seems to involve the Earth's magnetic field, whose strength pulses to a lunar rhythm and, like the tides, becomes strongest when the moon is directly overhead or below. We now know that plants are exquisitely electro-sensitive organisms, so it is likely that they are detecting this electric flux. As we unravel the plant's mysteries we may be close to finding an explanation for what the ancients seemed to know intuitively. As if by confirmation, recent experiments have shown that forest seedlings and radishes sown at the full moon germinate more quickly than those sown at other times. Other experiments have generated more questions than answers. The popular tropical fish, the guppy, has been shown to change its colour vision in time with the lunar cycle, seeing hues differently at various phases of the moon. No one quite knows why.

Earthquake Prediction

The moon has one other important influence on Earth; it creates tides in the Earth's crust. As the moon passes overhead, the Earth bulges towards it. Twice each day, Moscow rides an earth wave 0.5 metres high. Similarly, like some giant squeezebox, Europe and North America are pulled together by 20 metres and then pushed apart. As the Earth breathes with this lunar rhythm it can be triggered into turmoil. As rocks are put under stress and finally fracture the results can be catastrophic. More earthquakes occur around the full and new moons than at any other time. And as if by some innate ability for precognition many animals seem able to predict their arrival.

Earthquakes are one the most unpredictable and damaging of all natural events but throughout history it has been believed that animals can foretell their imminent devastation. Snakes leave their underground retreats, cats carry kittens out of houses, horses stampede, birds call in alarm and rats leave buildings and run around the streets. In China, in the 1980s, a million people were saved from an earthquake through the simple observation of strange animal behaviour. But interpretation is a difficult art and a year later a similar quake went undetected. Even so, animals in Tokyo Zoo are regularly monitored in case they give clues to impending quakes.

From what we know of the varied powers of animals, they might be reacting to many potential warning signs. Some may simply be physical; a rise in the water table may drive snakes and rodents out of their underground retreats. They may also pick up sounds missed by human observers. Birds would hear deep infrasound produced by the low rumbling of earth tremors, as would zoo animals such as elephants. Many vibration-sensitive animals, including spiders, scorpions and snakes, would also detect the tiny earth movements that might presage a quake. Groundwater, in a fault under extreme pressure, separates into electrically charged particles that might electrolyse chemicals to produce gases that animals may also detect.

But one of the main clues to the mystery could be the eerie earthlights some-times reported before a quake. These ghostly apparitions might be caused by intense ionization of the air as rock creates electrostatic charges when it twists and buckles under the strain. We now know that animals have the power to respond to this ionization. The same severe stresses would also create fluctuations in the local magnetic field of the Earth, to which animals appear equally sensitive.

We are at the edge of understanding how many of these hidden forces are used by other life, but the deeper we look the more it seems that ancient observations about the apparently SuperNatural powers of animals were largely correct. Their extrasensory abilities make them acutely sensitive to the subtlest shifts in the hidden forces that surround us.

Away from the sensory realm, in the world of the purely physical, animals and plants have equally remarkable powers, which we consider in the next chapter.

4

OUTER LIMITS

Among the SuperNatural powers possessed by animals are those that push physical endurance to the limit. Many forms of life can cope with conditions that would test the human body to destruction; surviving extremes of heat or cold would soon extinguish our life processes. Some can survive pressures so high that they would crush our body to a pulp, while others can withstand pressures so low we would need a space suit to survive. Some can live without a continuous supply of oxygen or in toxic concentrations of chemicals. Others can go without food and water for almost inconceivable periods of time.

If we possessed any of these powers we would regard them as SuperNatural, but the way animals achieve these superhuman feats is no less remarkable. Some of the new discoveries about these organisms, living at the outer limits of existence, have even begun to unravel some of the mysteries of life outside our planet.

Previous pages
Male emperor penguins
huddle together
against the icy blast
of the Arctic winter
where temperatures
can drop below -60°C.
In this natural deep
freeze, males incubate
their eggs, surviving
for four months with-
out feeding.

The Burning Bush

Of all the elemental forces on Earth, fire is perhaps the most primal. It is still a focus of human fascination and the centrepiece of most mystical and religious rituals. In the natural world its power is no less important and for several organisms it is a vital part of their existence.

Some plants have such a passion for fire that they actually set themselves alight. The aromatic garden plant dittany, mentioned in Chapter 2, is also called the burning bush because of its tendency to spontaneous combustion. It has a pungent lemony smell that emanates from oil glands on its leaves and, on a still day, these heavy vapours veil the plant. They are so inflammable that the slightest spark, perhaps from a stone kicked by a wild animal, causes this volatile halo to ignite. Because of this weird phenomenon fire-worshippers in India considered the plant sacred.

Another incendiary plant, *Cistus creticus*, is found in the Middle East and may be behind the Biblical story of the burning bush. Like dittany, this shrub creates volatile oils that ignite when exposed to a spark. The flames burn out competitors and stimulate the plants' seeds to crack open. The seeds, now permeable to water and oxygen and fertilized by the nutrients released through burning, soon start to grow. Many other seeds, particularly Mediterranean species, need to experience intense fire before they will germinate.

The seeds of many other plants need to be exposed to smoke in order to germinate. In the fynbos heathlands of South Africa, over half the plants, including the spectacular protea flower, need this kind of fumigation. The smoke prompts the seeds to germinate at a time when the soil is rich in nutrients and the competition has been burnt away.

As fire maintains many environments, it is now believed that the vegetation that grows there is often responsible for causing the periodic conflagrations that sweep through the landscape. In Australia the heavy oils that hang in a blue haze over the eucalyptus forests are easily combustible and play a role in creating the fires that burn out the competition. The trees themselves are generally resistant to these fast-moving flames.

People tend to see fire as a threat both to the landscape and to their own interests, so most early fire-control measures were directed at preventing fires from breaking out. The result, when the land finally burst into flames, was intense catastrophic infernos, not normally found in nature, which destroyed both vegetation and many human lives. A more enlightened policy now features prescribed burns, which try to emulate the fast-burning fires that, in nature, regularly refresh the environment.

Joining the human fire-fighters at many wild fires or prescribed burns are creatures with an unusual fascination for flames.

Fire Beetles

Melanophila beetles have a strange yearning – a burning desire to find fire.

Usually they live alone, widely dispersed across the landscape, but when fire erupts, hundreds magically appear together in the afterglow. Their apparent pyromania has a purpose: their larvae consume freshly burnt wood so, when a forest fire breaks out, they race to be first at the blaze. The beetles are in such a hurry to lay their eggs in the freshly charred timber that they often arrive in the middle of the blaze and may even bite fire-fighters in their excitement. How they find the fire so quickly has only recently been discovered.

Melanophila has two special sensors sunk in pits on its thorax at the base of each middle leg. Each pit contains a hundred sensory domes that warp when they sense flames. They react to wavelengths longer than the darkest red our eyes can see. Although most of this infrared is quickly absorbed, fortunately for the beetles a window in the atmosphere lets through a narrow band of this invisible light. The beetles are so attuned to this ribbon of infrared that they can react to a blaze burning 50 kilometres away.

Desiccated Animals

Although not as spectacular as sensory pyromania, equally remarkable is the ability of some creatures to withstand the prolonged exposure to heat that causes them to dry out completely.

Some of the most transient environments on earth are the pools that form on barren rock surfaces in northern Nigeria and Uganda. They can exist only for a brief period after rain and, almost as soon as they are formed, the searing sun burns down like a blowtorch and starts the process of evaporation again.

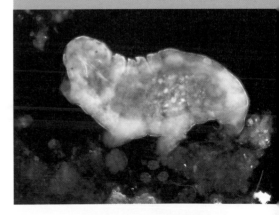

This tiny creature, known as a tardigrade or water bear, can survive total desiccation for over a hundred years.

Remarkably the larvae of a midge known as *Polypedilum* manages to survive here. As the water evaporates, the fly larva begins to enter a state of suspended animation. Water is sucked from its body until less than 3 per cent remains. In this desiccated state, it can endure temperatures as high as 70°C while it waits for the life-giving deluge of the next rainfall.

Among the several other creatures able to survive total dehydration are the tiny, eight-legged organisms called tardigrades, also known as water bears because they lumber around with a bear-like gait. They are found almost everywhere but, as the biggest are only the size of a pinhead, their interesting ursine locomotion is rarely noticed.

Fire is one of the most
primal forces on Earth,
but with the destruction
it causes comes life.
The proteus flower
(above) needs to be
stimulated by smoke
before its seeds will
germinate.

When their environment dries out, they form a protective envelope around themselves and shut down their metabolism completely. In this state they can be immersed in brine, ether, absolute alcohol or even liquid helium, and still survive. The temperature may soar to 149°C or drop to -272°C: it makes no difference to these miniature bears in their tiny protective dens. To the outside world they might as well be dead, but just add water and they gradually start to swell and magically come alive. They have been known to resurrect themselves 120 years after the life was last sucked out of them.

With some creatures, only their egg stages are able to survive total desiccation. The miniature crustaceans known as brine shrimps produce eggs that can dehydrate until their water content is just 10 per cent. In this state they can survive for 10,000 years.

Such survival periods seem almost inconceivable, but only a few specialist lower organisms have this ability. Among the higher animals, the ability to survive entombed for long periods of time is the stuff of myths and legends.

Toad in the Hole

Throughout history there have been reports of toads, discovered by builders, surviving unharmed entombed inside walls. Because the date when the structures were built was generally known, it became accepted that toads could miraculously live holed up for thirty years or more. In Victorian times an inquisitive scientist put the theory to the test in a series of experiments that trapped toads inside various cavities. Needless to say the hapless toads all died within a few months.

Nevertheless, the phenomenon seemed real enough, so how did the toads come to be found there? The most likely explanation is that they entered the wall as toadlets, while still small enough to squeeze through a crack to the cavity inside. The chamber would provide shelter and high humidity and, because insects were attracted by the same conditions, the toad would have a ready supply of food. Before long the amphibian would grow too big to escape, but it could still be sustained from insects taking refuge from outside.

These toads would need a certain amount of luck and a regular supply of food to survive their entombment, but the amount of folklore regarding this phenomenon suggests that many have. Amazingly, there are some species of frog that are adapted for just this kind of incarceration.

In the desert regions of Australia it may not rain for ten years, but frogs still manage to thrive there. They sit out the drought hidden in a chamber a metre underground and wrapped in a cocoon of shed skin. The catholic frog and the flat-headed frog can both enter this dormant phase and, when they do, their bladders become huge water stores that may last them for seven years or more. In the past, Aborigines have used these frogs, which resemble water-filled balls, as a source of emergency refreshment in the desert. As soon as the first rains wet the ground the frogs miraculously reappear and the desert becomes a cacophony of their croaking calls.

There are even fish that possess similar powers. The lungfish are an ancient group found in Africa, Australia and South America. Because they live in rivers that regularly dry out, they breathe air through lungs rather than gills. While other fish flounder in the drying river mud, the lungfish escapes by burrowing downwards, swallowing mud as it travels and passing it out through its gills. Eventually, it creates a chamber, curls up and starts to secrete mucus. When the mucus dries the fish creates a protective cocoon around itself and an opening to the surface allows it to breathe air. As it passes away the arid months its metabolism drops and the little energy it needs comes from the breakdown of muscle tissue. In this state it can survive four to five years, but usually it simply has to sit out a single dry season.

Australian desert frogs can survive for several years underground waiting for a drought to end. They are used as emergency water supplies by Aborigines.

Eaten Alive

Being buried alive may seem a fate worse than death, but being eaten alive is a fate that almost any animal would also avoid. Remarkably there is one that seeks out this experience.

The revena weevil feeds on the seeds of the palm-nut tree and lays its eggs on the developing fruit. When the larvae hatch they burrow down into the seeds as the fruit develops and ripens. Toucans eat the fruits, but far from being a disaster for the weevil grubs, this is the moment they have been waiting for. Although most of the swallowed fruit is broken down in the bird's stomach, within thirty minutes the seeds are regurgitated. Most of the grubs survive this hazardous journey and when the seed is spat out they almost immediately disembark to burrow down into the soil, metamorphosing into an adult weevil four months later.

This unorthodox journey is actually an effective means of dispersal for the weevil, as foraging toucans spend only a few minutes at each palm-nut tree before they move on.

G Force

Another bizarre feat of endurance is shown by those animals that willingly subject themselves to extreme physical forces.

We, like all other organisms, are kept on the Earth by the force of gravity. To escape the Earth's gravitational pull, rockets generate forces four times greater than the gravitational pull (4 G). G forces higher than that are experienced by fighter pilots, but at around 7 G most people pass out.

Under extreme conditions of momentary impact people have survived devastating G forces. A driver in a racing car has been recorded as decelerating from 173 kilometres an hour to zero over a distance of just 66 centimetres as he crashed into a wall, experiencing 179.8 G in the process. He suffered twenty-nine fractures and six heart stoppages as a result, but ultimately he survived. In daily life, woodpeckers regularly submit themselves to G forces far in excess of this.

When a woodpecker drills its bill against the trunk of a tree to find food or to proclaim its territory it is subjecting itself to devastating impacts. As it drums, its bill is driven into the wood at a speed of 700 centimetres per second and, at the moment of impact, it experiences forces of between 600 and 1500 G. So how does the woodpecker survive its daily dose of head-banging?

Because woodpeckers have relatively smaller brains than we do, the impact is scaled down, making them around fifty times less susceptible to damage than we are. Because their brain contains little of the cerebrospinal fluid that surrounds our brains, the hazardous shock waves are not transmitted so easily either. The woodpecker also employs some inventive structural engineering: the beak is positioned below the brain cavity to prevent impact forces transmitting directly to the brain and the skull is also reinforced, particularly at the point where the bill attaches to the skull. In addition, muscles attached to the bill contract just before impact and act as shock absorbers.

Among the woodpecker's prey are creatures that show a similar impressive tolerance to G forces. The click beetle experiences these extreme forces while making its escape. Its surprise defence involves jack-knifing into the air when attacked. To make the jump it arches its back, tensing a spine that catches on the underside of its body. As the tension increases the spine springs from the catch with a loud click. This propels the beetle, at an incredible rate of acceleration, nearly 30 centimetres into the air. At peak velocity it can experience up to 500 G. This death-defying pogo-ing startles any predator, causing it to jump back in alarm and giving the click beetle a chance to escape.

Birds that hunt by swooping down on their prey also have to tolerate huge forces. Plummeting earthwards, a peregrine, wings swept back to form an air-slicing arrow, may reach almost 300 kilometres an hour. As it knocks its prey out of the sky or

The amazing click beetle can experience a force of 500 G as it propels itself into the air. This stunt-leaping startles any predator.

When a brown pelican dives into the water, its breast withstands shock waves that can stun a fish 2 metres away.

approaches the ground, it can pull out of the descent almost instantly. Human test pilots would black out under these manoeuvres, but the peregrine recovers instantly.

Although brown pelicans are not nearly so fast as peregrines, they take their prey by plunge diving and need to endure the impact that forces them through the water surface. They often target fish from 10 metres above and drop down on them with wings swept back. Although the bill hits the water first, the breast takes most of the impact, creating a shock wave that can stun fish 2 metres away. Air sacs under the skin on the front of the body protect the pelican from serious damage.

The gannet has refined its plunge-diving technique. It drops on shoals of fish from heights of up to 30 metres and, by folding its wings into a V, it becomes as stream-lined as an arrow, reaching 100 kilometres an hour by the time it hits the water. Its aerodynamic shape helps it cut through water as readily as air, reducing the damage caused by the impact.

Speed Freaks

Because birds fly through a relatively frictionless environment, they reach the highest speeds of any creatures. Those that live on land need to overcome the drag created by contact with the ground. Even so, some land mammals reach awesome speeds.

The cheetah is renowned for being the fastest animal on Earth but even now the speed at which it can run is widely disputed. The highest estimates claim speeds of an unbelievable 144 kilometres an hour, the lowest suggest a meagre 70. The truth appears to lie somewhere in between – around 100 kilometres an hour is the most commonly agreed estimate. Even more remarkably, the cheetah reaches this top speed in just three seconds. But it pays a price in high-speed chases. It builds up massive quantities of heat, raising its body temperature to 40.6°C. This temperature is just under fatal levels. If the chases were any more prolonged, the cheetah would die from heat stroke.

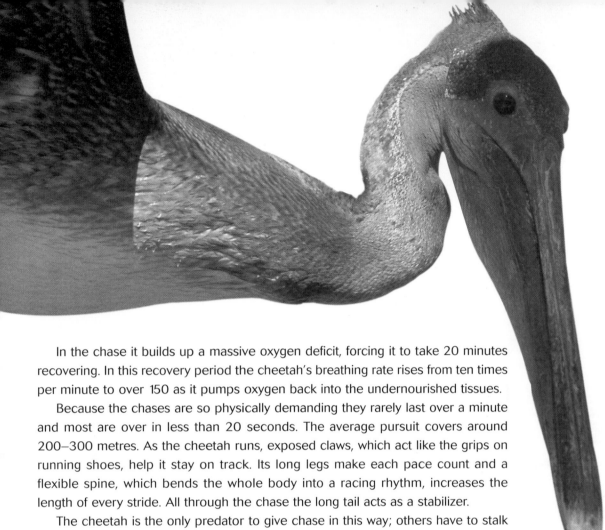

In the chase it builds up a massive oxygen deficit, forcing it to take 20 minutes recovering. In this recovery period the cheetah's breathing rate rises from ten times per minute to over 150 as it pumps oxygen back into the undernourished tissues.

Because the chases are so physically demanding they rarely last over a minute and most are over in less than 20 seconds. The average pursuit covers around 200–300 metres. As the cheetah runs, exposed claws, which act like the grips on running shoes, help it stay on track. Its long legs make each pace count and a flexible spine, which bends the whole body into a racing rhythm, increases the length of every stride. All through the chase the long tail acts as a stabilizer.

The cheetah is the only predator to give chase in this way; others have to stalk close to their prey to stand a chance of catching it.

Inevitably, the cheetah's prey has to be nearly as fleet of foot, and the Thompson's gazelle has been clocked at 94 kilometres an hour, but the fastest animal capable of prolonged running is the American antelope, which set the land-speed record by maintaining 88 kilometres an hour for 800 metres.

World Travellers

The speed freaks have their endurance counterparts; these are the animals that spend their lives making incredible journeys. The swift is renowned for spending a year of its life aloft, sleeping on the wing and coming back to earth only to breed. On an average day it flies almost 1000 kilometres and in a year it can clock up a staggering 400,000 kilometres. If it made the same journey vertically upwards it would reach the moon.

Swallows are similar long-distance travellers. When they return from Africa to Europe in April, they have completed a round trip of 20,000 kilometres. When feeding trips are included, the total distance the bird flies in the half year spent away can be as much as 300,000 kilometres.

In the chase a cheetah may reach as much as 100 kilometres an hour. Such high-octane performance takes its toll: its body temperature is raised to near-lethal levels and it acquires a massive oxygen deficit. Recovery from the exertion takes at least 20 minutes.

An albatross, on a single feeding trip – which usually lasts around a month – may cover over 14,000 kilometres without ever touching the ground; it lets the air currents take the strain, soaring on the uplift of air produced by the ocean waves with scarcely a wingbeat.

In terms of straight distance, no bird can compete with the Arctic tern. It breeds as far north as the Arctic Circle but overwinters on the edge of the Antarctic ice pack – a straight-line distance of about 15,000 kilometres. The complete migratory round trip could be as much as 40,000 kilometres, the equivalent of circumnavigating the globe. The oldest ringed Arctic tern was 26 years old, so it is likely that it flew a world-shrinking million kilometres in its lifetime.

Birds are not the only long-distance travellers. Grey whales make journeys of between 12,000 and 20,000 kilometres each year and turtles regularly travel 10,000 kilometres on their migrations. All these creatures need to use energy to make their incredible journeys, but some smaller organisms travel similar distances with no effort whatsoever.

High Life

Many small invertebrates are accomplished aeronauts, ascending into the sky and drifting on the wind to find new worlds. There is such a wealth of life sailing around on air currents that, on the high snow fields and glaciers of our tallest mountains, creatures eke out a living from the aerial cargo that showers down on them like manna from heaven. As many as six insects a day may fall on a single square metre of snow and, among the reception party, living far above the normal reaches of life, are jumping spiders and the ancient group of insects known as bristletails and springtails.

As well as the risk of becoming marooned on hostile ice fields, animals that disperse on the wind face other severe problems. Once they reach altitudes of 5 kilometres, temperatures fall below -20°C, instantly turning any water to ice. To survive, some spiders and aphids contain super-cooling agents that allow them to sail the high-altitude winds in a state of suspended animation.

The tiny spiders often known as money spiders are among these well-prepared aeronauts. When conditions are favourable, the spiderlings climb up stems, leaves or rocks and wait for a passing gust of wind. They then ply a thread of silk to catch the breeze. As they are wafted upwards, the silken line acts as a sail, and the spiders can even control the rate of ascent by adjusting its length. If the spiderlings eventually reach the jet stream, they may journey for thousands of kilometres before descending; at times they may orbit the world. To protect themselves from ultraviolet rays and help soak up the heat, their bodies are black, but even when temperatures are so low that ice crystals form on the hair on their bodies, they manage to survive.

The most remarkable of all aeronauts are the tiny microbial algae that populate the oceans of the world. Recent research suggests that these microscopic plants can manipulate the weather to create conditions that can transport them across the globe. The secret of this extraordinary climatic tampering lies in a substance produced by the algae, known as DMS, which acts as a seed for cloud formation. As the clouds develop above the sea, they trigger upwelling currents of hot air that the algae use as elevators. Once in the clouds, they are transported around the world by the weather systems they helped create.

Bird Aeronauts

Making use of these weather systems are migrating birds. Some travel to incredible altitudes. Dunlin, knot and other small migrating birds have regularly been recorded at heights of 7000 metres, well into the lanes of commercial airlines. One pilot flying over the Outer Hebrides at 8200 metres found a flock of migrating whooper swans sharing his air space. Remarkably, some birds even enter the inhospitable zone known as the stratosphere – the layer of thin atmosphere between 10 and 50 kilometres above the earth. Bar-headed geese have been spotted crossing the Himalayas at heights of 9000 metres, close to where the stratosphere begins. The high-altitude prize is held by an unfortunate but record-breaking Ruppell's griffon vulture, which collided with an aircraft an incredible 12 kilometres above the earth.

Bar-headed geese have been spotted at heights of 9000 metres, an altitude that takes them into the flight paths of aircraft. Such high-flying birds have been mistaken for hostile fighter planes.

At this height, concentrations of oxygen are less than a third of what they are at sea level. To cope with these low levels of oxygen geese and other birds have highly efficient forms of the oxygen-carrying molecule haemoglobin in their blood, and a high density of blood capillaries to transport this oxygen to their flight muscles. How they endure the cold is more of a mystery. At this height, temperatures may drop to below -50°C and migrating birds may spend several days in these freezing conditions.

Close to the poles, such intense cold can be a daily part of life. It is here that the real cold specialists are found.

Cold Comfort

In the Arctic regions of the world it is not uncommon for animals regularly to endure temperatures below -70°C. Mammals that survive here employ several strategies to fight the glacial conditions. Musk ox rely on the ultimate fur coat. Their thick shag-pile covering has an underfur eight times warmer than sheep's wool and is such an efficient insulator that snow accumulates on the animal's back. Even when outside temperatures drop to -40°C the musk ox still manages to maintain a constant body temperature of about 38°C. If it gets colder they have their own internal heater, burning stored fat to generate warmth.

Like the musk ox, the Arctic fox uses a thick winter coat to keep itself snug. It, too, has an inner lining of fine underfur and it even has fur on the soles of its feet to protect them from frostbite. It can also reduce the blood flow to its skin, conserving body warmth. The fox is so protected that it needs to burn its fat reserves to generate heat only when temperatures drop below -50°C.

Perhaps unsurprisingly, polar bears are the supreme cold-weather animal. Their underfur consists of a thick duvet of dense wool covered by a mattress-thick layer of hollow guard hairs which stay erect and provide insulation even when wet. They also have an insulating layer of blubber over their back legs and lower back which is as thick as twenty blankets.

The polar bear has such perfect insulation that it almost disappears when observed with a heat-sensitive camera. Only the nose and part of the upper back show any sign of giving off warmth and, because these bears also lose heat through their pads and claws, their tracks leave behind a glowing imprint. At rest the polar bear gives off no more heat than a 200-watt light bulb.

With such efficient insulation, even in intense cold, an active bear easily overheats. Ironically, the polar bear spends much of its time trying to cool down. To lose excess heat its heart pumps more blood to its footpads and claws and also to its snout and legs. It can also shunt blood to a radiator, made of two sheets of thin muscle across its back, if it still fails to cool down.

Polar bears are so perfectly insulated from the cold that they spend most of the time trying to cool down.

If, despite these cooling techniques, the bear's core temperature rises above 38.7°C, its heartbeat increases from a resting pulse of about 45 per minute to a high of 148. At the same time, it starts to breathe rapidly and shallowly to bring cool air to its lungs.

Because mammals have the ability to control their body temperature they are ideally suited for life in the freezer. Reptiles, with their body temperature linked to the outside world, are usually confined to warm climates. Even so, some live in surprisingly cold places and show a remarkable ability to survive refrigeration.

The Chinese alligator inhabits a region where winter temperatures frequently fall below zero. As it is slowly enveloped by river ice, the alligator keeps the tip of its snout exposed, despite the rest of its head and body becoming totally immobilized. In this trapped state it survives until the spring thaw.

Red-sided garter snakes are among the world's most cold-resistant reptiles. Their skills are frequently tested at their hibernation sites at Narcisse, near Winnipeg in Manitoba, Canada. The snakes overwinter in cavities eroded out of the limestone bedrock. Relatively few of these overwintering dens exist, but those that do attract tens of thousands of snakes. In spring they fill the entrances of these natural snake pits with their writhing bodies. Because summers are so short at these northerly latitudes, the snakes make every day count by emerging at the first sign of spring.

The males are the first to appear and soon the snake pit becomes a heaving mass of serpents waiting for the females to come to the surface. When the first females finally emerge they may be outnumbered by as much as 10,000 to one and are soon consumed in a squirming mating ball of amorous males.

The battle between the males for first call on the females forces them to take dangerous gambles with the weather. Spring days, which rapidly turn from sun to snow showers, produce plummeting temperatures. As their body temperature drops the snakes become increasingly sluggish and the journey back to the den turns into a race against the thermometer.

At this time of year, many snakes are trapped in the icy grip of unexpected blizzards and, by nightfall, their bodies have become freeze-dried into ice sculptures. But, as the morning sunshine thaws the snow, something miraculous happens – the snakes slowly, almost imperceptibly at first, come back to life. Their tolerance to an occasional spell in the deep freeze is the only way they can survive in these northern regions. But if the bad weather lasts more than a day they can be in trouble – they can tolerate this freeze-packed state for a maximum of twenty-four hours.

Insects that live in high northern regions face similar weather problems and the short Arctic summer means that their active life has to be squeezed into a few weeks of the year. Because of this, the Arctic moth of Greenland and northern Canada has one of the most protracted life-cycles of all insects, taking thirteen years to complete. Its spurt of growth is confined to June and each day it feeds for just a few hours around midday. By the end of June, summer is over and the caterpillars stop feeding and seek shelter. They are forced by the hardness of the permafrost to overwinter close to the surface, which means they are exposed to the full force of the Arctic winter. They freeze at about -7°C and remain frozen for up to nine months of the year, surviving temperatures as low as -100°C. The ice that forms in their bodies cuts their cells to shreds, but when they thaw out in the spring they soon repair the damage.

Many birds show remarkable tolerance to cold. Even small passerines, such as goldfinches and siskins, are surprisingly tolerant to a brief spell in nature's deep freeze. Even if the outside temperature drops to -70°C they still manage to maintain a normal body temperature for several hours. Such cold tolerance must help migrating birds endure the temperatures they encounter at altitude.

Emperor penguins are among the hardiest birds on the planet, choosing the heart of the Antarctic winter to breed. All other life migrates away to avoid temperatures that drop below -60°C and winds that cut like icy razors at speeds of 200 kilometres per hour. Although the females leave, the male emperor penguins stoically stay behind and for a period of two months or so they incubate a single egg, most of the time in total darkness. The eggs are well protected from the cold, raised off the icy surface by the penguin's feet and tucked into a brood pouch. The penguin's only protection comes from the massed bodies of other birds; 6000 of them may huddle together for warmth, taking it in turns to enter the inner scrum. While they endure the Arctic weather they show another remarkable ability – they refrain from eating throughout the entire chilling experience.

Fasting

While male emperor penguins incubate their eggs they may survive for as long as 120 days without a morsel of food. They exist on reserves of subcutaneous fat and, by the time they have returned to the open ocean, they are half the penguin they once were.

Polar bears can endure even longer periods of fasting. When the sea ice melts in June, around the Hudson Bay area of Canada, pregnant females trek hundreds of kilometres to their breeding grounds, where they carve out an underground chamber in the snow. In this cosy den, they give birth to cubs and pass away the Arctic winter. For eight whole months they go without food, relying on stored fat to nourish them and their growing cubs. Every day they lose 1 kilogram of their body food store and by the time winter is over they will be 200 kilograms lighter. Their fast comes to an end only once they reach their hunting grounds the following March or April.

Predators need the greatest endurance because they can never be certain where the next meal is coming from. Among fish, sharks are capable of the longest periods of fasting. A swell shark has been known to survive fifteen months without a meal.

Breath-holding

Going without oxygen tests another aspect of an animal's stamina. Some creatures can live without any oxygen whatsoever. The tapeworm, like many parasites, breathes anaerobically (without oxygen) in the oxygen-depleted contents of the intestine. Others, like the larvae of the bot fly that lives in the flesh of mammals, create their own oxygen supply by breaking down their body sugars into fat and breathing the oxygen that this process releases. But among animals that are designed to breathe atmospheric air some show extreme levels of endurance.

Opposite As winter, approaches, the fur of the Arctic fox turns white and develops a fine insulating underfur. Even the soles of its feet are covered with fur to avoid frostbite.

Weddell seals can hold their breath for over an hour. They perform this feat by storing oxygen in their blood and muscle and dropping their heart rate to just a few beats per minute.

Unsurprisingly, it is marine mammals that have taken breath holding to the ultimate. Although seals usually stay under the water for less than 30 minutes, many dives have been recorded as lasting more than an hour, including a Weddell seal that stayed submerged for 73 minutes. But the award for breath holding goes to the elephant seal, which has been recorded as staying down for two whole hours.

How do seals achieve such feats of endurance? Paradoxically, instead of taking a deep breath before they dive, they actually exhale, reducing the amount of oxygen in their lungs. While our blood makes up 7 per cent of our body weight, a seal carries proportionately twice this amount, and not only does it have more blood, its corpuscles, which contain oxygen-carrying haemoglobin, are also larger. In fact, a seal stores five times as much oxygen in the same amount of blood as a human. It also has a secondary oxygen store in its muscles, which humans lack. High concentrations of the oxygen-attracting molecule myoglobin give the meat of seals its characteristic deep red colour.

Even with all this extra capacity, a diving seal still needs to conserve oxygen. It does this by restricting the flow of blood to its stomach, muscles, skin and flippers by 90 per cent, leaving only the supply to the brain unaffected. To cope with the lack of oxygen it also reduces its heart rate from an average of 120 beat per minute to a barely alive two beats per minute. In a grey seal, this heart-stopping moment may last as long as 60 seconds and over this period, even though it should be dead, it still manages to chase and catch its prey.

Whales also regularly hold their breath for long periods. For sperm whales the average time below is 30–40 minutes but, like the elephant seal, they have been recorded as staying under for nearly two hours.

Instead of simply holding their breath, the white Arctic whales known as belugas use amazing sensory powers to survive under water. The males make migrations of 800 kilometres under solid pack ice to visit eating places 550 metres below the ice. But as a beluga's lungs are no bigger than those of a human, and its maximum breath-holding time is around 20 minutes, it has been difficult to understand how it achieves these feats. The secret appears to involve listening out for the character-istic slopping sound made as water hits a hole in the ice. At each dive a beluga may travel 2 kilometres before it hears the location of one of these breathing stops. To avoid getting caught out, it must always save enough air to return to their last breath-ing hole in an emergency.

Reptiles naturally have a low metabolism, which means they need little oxygen in order to stay alive – the earless lizard, found in North America, is reputed to be able to survive a day without oxygen. Because of this low rate of living, aquatic reptiles have an inbuilt advantage when staying underwater for extended periods.

Although crocodiles normally remain submerged for only a few minutes, they can easily stay under for more than an hour, and an American alligator, under duress, survived submersion for over six hours.

Birds have far higher metabolic rates; even so emperor penguins have been recorded as staying submerged for 18 minutes. On these dives they may reach depths of over 450 metres. This may seem an incredible feat for a bird, but air-breathing mammals dive to far greater depths.

Under Pressure

Grey seals descend to 400 metres, Weddell seals to 600, but the elephant seal holds the seals' deep-diving record, reaching a crushing depth of 1500 metres. How do these animals cope with such horrendous pressure?

Fortunately, most of the seal's body is solid and incompressible. The only chambers that can be crushed are those normally filled with air, and they are designed to take the strain. As the seal dives, water pressure on its flexible rib cage pushes air from the lungs and at the same time the trachea becomes compressed until it is half its normal volume. At depth, only a little air remains in the system.

Unlike divers, seals never experience the 'bends'. This condition occurs when nitrogen, forced into the blood under the pressure of depth, suddenly effervesces into the body tissues when the diver releases the pressure by returning quickly to the surface. Because animals take their air from the surface, rather than breathing pressurized air at depth, they do not encounter this dangerous effect.

Of all cetaceans, the sperm whale dives the deepest, regularly reaching depths of 400–600 metres. Some, however, have been recorded 2000 metres below the ocean surface and at their lower limit they are believed to plunge 3000 metres into the abyss. Leatherback turtles have been recorded at a depth of 1200 metres and their pursuit of dense shoals of jellyfish is believed to take them 1500 metres down.

Between 200 and 1000 metres is the area known as the mesopelagic zone, a dark world of strange luminous fish, shrimps and cone jellies. The denizens of this twilight zone are adapted to extreme pressures and rapidly die if brought to the surface. At depths below 1000 metres the ocean is in perpetual darkness. Weird-looking fish, very different from those at the surface, inhabit this eerie realm – among them dragon fish, viper fish, deep-sea eels, sharks and lemon-backed squid. The strange angler fish is found here, too. Its body is decorated with protuberances that act like bait and the females carry the males around with them, living parasitically off their bodies.

Some 6000 metres down lies the abyssal plain. A body falling from the surface would take two days to reach this underworld. But still life survives here, much of it

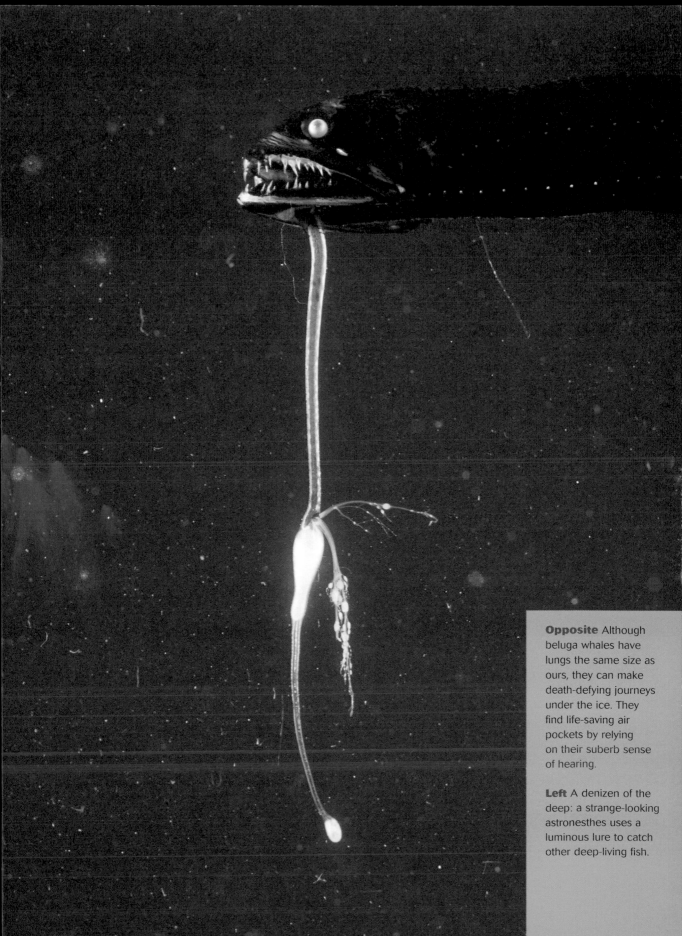

Opposite Although beluga whales have lungs the same size as ours, they can make death-defying journeys under the ice. They find life-saving air pockets by relying on their suberb sense of hearing.

Left A denizen of the deep: a strange-looking astronesthes uses a luminous lure to catch other deep-living fish.

feeding on the corpses that fall in a slow rain from the world above. Among these scavengers are hagfish, the deep-sea equivalent to vultures, which descend in swarms on any body that makes it to the bottom.

Occasionally, volcanic openings erupt from the seabed, spewing noxious chemicals and heat into the cold water. These toxic dumps attract some of the most extreme forms of life known on the planet.

Toxic Life

Volcanic vents form where plates in the earth's crust are slowly spreading apart. As cracks appear, water pours into the crevices up to 3 kilometres below the surface until they hit the scalding rocks beneath. Enriched by minerals from the rock, the super-heated water is forced back to the seabed through vents.

Scientists once thought that no living things could survive the harsh combination of toxic chemicals, high temperatures, high pressures and complete darkness around these vents, but in fact they are rapidly colonized by a bizarre community of SuperNatural creatures, of which over 300 different varieties have been discovered so far. The most conspicuous are giant tubeworms. These grow at nearly a metre a year and the red plumes that fan out from the end of the tubes soon decorate the area around the spewing vent like a field of swaying flowers. Besides the giant tubeworms there are a whole variety of lesser worms, including pen-sized Jericho worms, dark red palm worms with hairy fronds and orange worms decorated with tiny bristles. This toxic dump also attracts chemically tolerant shrimps, clams, mussels, crabs and even octopus.

Although water erupts from the vents at temperatures of up to 400°C, the scalding temperatures are confined to few centimetres around the vent opening; away from this the water temperature soon drops to a norm of just 2°C. So, to survive here, the main talents required are the abilities to endure high concentrations of toxic chemicals and to live in total darkness.

The main chemical is hydrogen sulphide, which smells of rotten eggs. Although toxic to most forms of life it is used as an energy source for the most important organisms of the deep-sea vents – bacteria.

Without bacteria none of the other creatures could survive. Even the eye-catching tubeworms are really housing developments for bacteria. The tubes are filled with brown spongy tissue into which are crammed 100 billion bacteria for every single gram. The tubeworm's red plumes are filled with blood that transports hydrogen sulphide, instead of oxygen, down to feed the bacteria. In return the bacteria oxidize the hydrogen sulphide and convert carbon dioxide into carbon compounds that nourish the worm.

There are even bacteria living in the super-heated water at the vent, where they withstand higher temperatures than any other living organism. These thermophilic microbes live at temperatures above 50°C. Not all are found in undersea vents – the volcanic hot springs at Yellowstone National Park in the United States have their own versions of thermophiles that tolerate temperatures of over 80°C. But the most heat-tolerant microbes of all are those that survive and grow in the boiling water of the deep-sea vents. Some even thrive at a pressure-cooking temperatures of 113°C.

Although the real heat specialists are bacteria, some higher forms of life can also tolerate extremes of temperature. A tiny crustacean known as a fairy shrimp pro-duces eggs that can be boiled alive without destroying the dormant life form inside.

Dormant forms of life, living in a state of suspended animation and resistant to the most extreme forces on earth, are also found among bacteria and fungi. Some may even survive a journey into outer space.

Microbial Astronauts

Leave a bowl of strawberries on your kitchen table or the lid off a jar of jam; leave a loaf of bread uneaten and a cup of tea undrunk and, in each case, you will breed a team of potential astronauts. Within a few days, moulds such as *Penicillium*, *Aspergillus* and *Mucor* miraculously start to grow on the food. Their sudden materi-alization occurs because their spores are specialized aeronauts that may begin their journey on another continent before they find their way to our kitchens. They can circumnavigate the globe, travelling at altitudes far higher than those reached by conventional aircraft.

The fungal spores are so small and light that they drift about on the slightest breeze, floating far up into the atmosphere. They, along with the spores of bacteria, have been found in the mesophere, at the limits of the atmosphere, where space begins. The fungal spores seem to be prepared for these journeys, as they contain protective dark pigments that guard against the extreme low temperatures and high levels of ultraviolet radiation found at these altitudes.

At this height, the next step of leaving our Earth and travelling into outer space is but a small one. The spores are so tiny that gravity has little effect on them, but because they hold an electrical charge they do react to the forces of electrical attraction and repulsion. Repelled by the Earth's magnetic field, they are launched away from the planet and upwards into interstellar space.

The vacuum of space and temperatures as low as -200°C presents no problem to the spores – they are able to live in this suspended state of animation for 7000 years or more. It is also quite possible that these long-distance interplanetary travellers could seed other planets with life.

Inset (above) Some like it hot. This heat-loving bacteria's natural home is a volcanic hot spring bubbling with sulphur. In this miniature Hades it can survive temperatures of 90° C.

Right The tranquil beauty of this blue pool in Yellowstone National Park in the USA belies the fact that it is one of the most inhospitable environments on earth. Only a few heat-loving bacteria survive the searing volcanic heat.

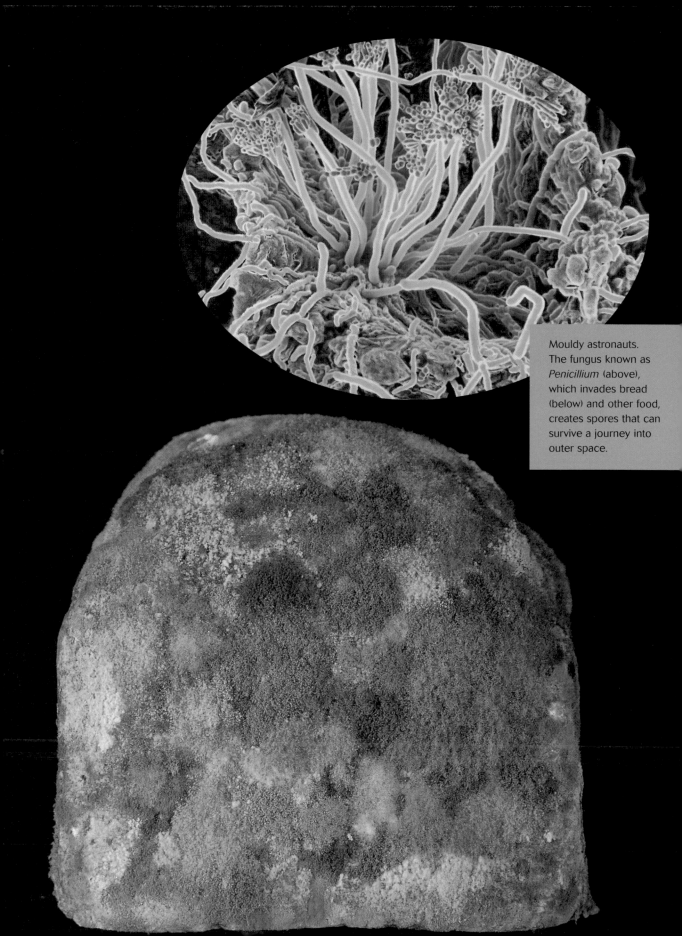

Mouldy astronauts. The fungus known as *Penicillium* (above), which invades bread (below) and other food, creates spores that can survive a journey into outer space.

Intraterrestrials

Fungal and bacterial spores may become Earth's extraterrestrial travellers but closer to home similar organisms that have just been discovered are being studied for their possible similarities to the life that may inhabit other planets. These intraterrestrials are found deep below the Earth's surface.

It was once believed that any subterranean life would need regular replenishment from the Earth's surface, thereby limiting the depths at which it could be found. But recently scientists have become more skilled at isolating samples and detecting traces of life and, no matter how deep they drill, their core samples still contain micro-organisms.

At levels above 100 metres, single-celled protozoans known as flagellates hunt the smaller bacterial intraterrestrials, swimming through the rock fissures and grazing on the bacterial harvest. Below 100 metres the bacteria have the rocks to themselves.

Early drillings down through sedimentary rocks at Savannah River in California found life 500 metres below the surface. Then cores taken through the sediment in every ocean found high populations of life at depths of 750 metres. As populations hardly declined with increasing depth, it seemed that life must exist far deeper.

In sediments life forms pervade the whole structure, squeezing their way into every pore. Some sediment extends 15 kilometres beneath the earth, providing a potential home for a huge biomass of living organisms. In solid igneous rock life is confined to the fissures, but even in granite it has been found 860 metres down. With such a huge volume of living space available, it is likely that life in the deep biosphere actually weighs more than all the life found at the surface.

The bacteria in sedimentary rock survive by consuming the remnants of prehistoric organic matter; to obtain oxygen, they break down the rusts of iron, sulphur and manganese. The bacteria are team players relying on each other for support. They break down the food in stages, one micro-organism's waste providing food for the next in the chain. Literally hundreds of different species, all adapted to their own specialist niches, survive in a co-operative spirit among the rocks.

More remarkably, life is also found in rocks that contain no organic remains of past life. Here, bacteria survive by actually eating the rock. They create their own food from dissolved hydrogen and carbon dioxide.

As if these rock-eaters were not weird enough, they are eclipsed by the heat-loving bacteria that have recently been found in gold mines. Living 3.5 kilometres beneath the surface, these act like miniature alchemists, secretly creating gold. As they feed on the rock, they cause the gold that is there to precipitate out and in the process the bacteria become dusted with microscopic gold fragments. It seems that these 22-carat bacteria are involved in laying down the gold in the seam, making them the most valuable micro-organisms on Earth.

Many of these intraterrestrial bacteria live at an incredibly slow rate – they divide as little as once every 100 years, compared with three times an hour for bacteria at the surface. Generations of these organisms have been living with no contact with the surface for millions, if not billions, of years.

Such time scales appear inconceivable to us, but our concept of time is unique to our species. Every other organism on Earth lives in its own special time world, as we shall see in Chapter 5.

Below Spores of a puffball fungus magnified 10,000 times.

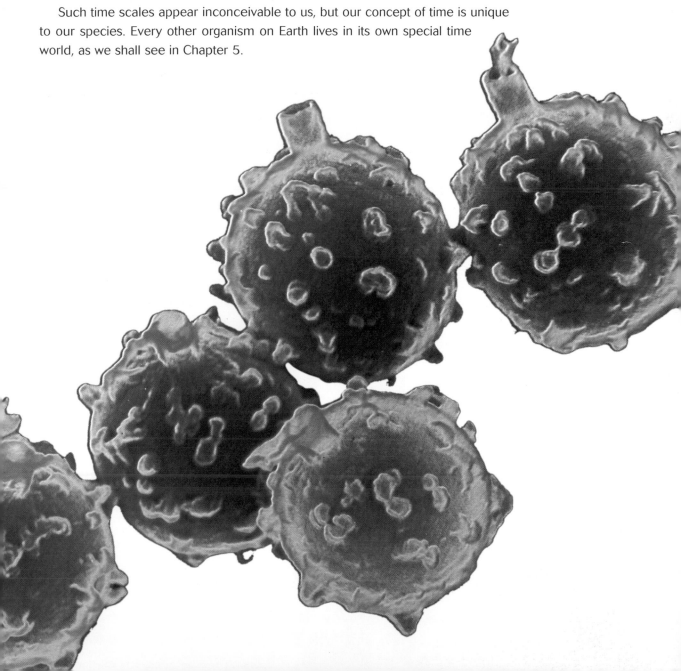

5

TIME WARP

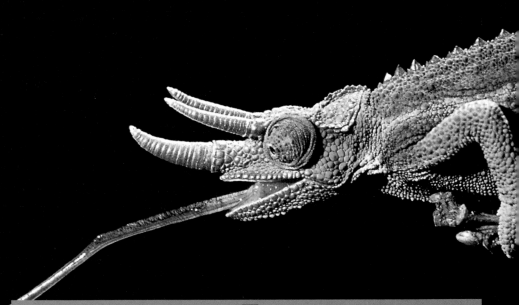

There is something intangible about time. Although we mark its progress with increasing precision, we still find it almost impossible to define. To add to the confusion, the passage of time sometimes seems to vary. If we suffer from a fever and our temperature is raised, time appears to pass more slowly. With the use of different drugs it can speed up or slow down. When we face life-threatening situations, such as a car crash, this time warping becomes almost paranormal; it is as though we have stretched the fabric of time.

Although we occasionally glimpse these different time worlds, other creatures exist in them all the time. Some have become time-stretching specialists, eking out seconds into what to them appear to be longer moments. Often these are predators – this time warping gives them the edge when pursuing fast-moving prey. Others play a waiting game, shrinking time to pass the empty hours. For reptiles and other cold-blooded animals, time is a continually variable experience, the minutes racing by when they are cold but slowing down into longer moments when they are warm and hunting prey.

Some creatures have mastered cryogenic techniques (the ability to survive at extraordinarily low temperatures) and opt out of periods of time altogether; others have found ways of skipping centuries or even millennia, effectively travelling through time.

How each organism perceives the passage of time is at the core of its existence but, although the perceptions of different species may vary, they still share the same way of ticking off the days. Life has a rhythm that beats to the daily cycle of light and darkness created by the sun. This daily pulse synchronizes the body clocks of almost all the plants and animals on the planet. And, as we saw in Chapter 3, the moon acts as a secondary timepiece for many animals and plants.

Flicker Fusion

Of all the various ways of perceiving time, one of the most extraordinary is the way different creatures register fast events in their eyes. If a blowfly buzzed into a cinema and looked up at the screen, its multi-faceted compound eye would gain only a fragmented version of the picture. If it ignored these distracting pixilations and continued to watch the film it would see a rapidly moving slide show rather than continuous flowing action. This difference between the fly's view and our own is due to its faster perception of time.

The movie industry relies on our slow resolution of images to merge a succession of static pictures and make them appear as continuous motion. The interval at which these separate images blend is known as our flicker-fusion frequency. This varies from about ten images per second in poor light to around fifty per second in good light. Although only twenty-four cinema frames are viewed each second, the projector shutter passes three times over every frame to ensure a smooth, flicker-free illusion of action.

The cinema fly, with a flicker-fusion frequency of 400, sees intervals of time between eight and twenty times shorter than we can. Such high-speed perception might mar a fly's enjoyment of Hollywood's fantasies, but when that fly faces real-life dramas these powers can make the difference between life and death, enabling it instantly to avoid the angry flick of a member of the audience's hand or any other attempts to swat it.

A cinema-going spider would appreciate the film more than the fly. Its flicker-fusion rate matches our own and so it, too, would see continuous action. But the spider's eyesight is poor, so details of scenes would be difficult to follow. This hardly matters to the orb spiders which trap high-speed prey in a web, but wolf spiders, which actively hunt their prey, have far better vision than their web-spinning relatives. Wolf spiders have been shown to have a genuine appreciation of the movies. By playing back images of their prey on television, scientists have provoked the kind of excited reaction from the spider that an Arnold Schwarzenegger block-buster generates in a teenage audience.

Stretching Time

Most insects see only a coarse, fragmented view of the world so, to experience their time world clearly, it would pay to become a dragonfly. This bulbous-eyed insect has more facets in its compound eye than any other and, because each of these increases visual definition, the dragonfly's 30,000 facets gives it a view of the world that we would recognize. But it also has a flicker-fusion frequency of 300, six times faster than ours — which would make a vast difference to our perception of high-speed events.

For instance, if it started to rain, rather than seeing falling streaks of water, our newly acquired sight would register each raindrop as a glistening sphere. As these globes hit the ground they would warp and collapse, then rise up again to form ephemeral glass-like crowns. As we walked, these growing and collapsing coronas would erupt from the paving stones beneath our feet and, around our heads, thou-sands more droplets would fall like glass beads. This beautiful view would be marred by the limited resolution of even the dragonfly's eye. The amount of detail that an insect's eye can gather is limited by its size; to match the resolution of our vision it would have to be scaled up to be a metre wide.

Birds have the best vision of any creature, far superior to our own. They not only see more detail and more colours than we can, they also have higher flicker-fusion rates. Of the limited number of birds that have been measured, chickens were shown to have a flicker-fusion frequency of 100 and pigeons 140, so it is likely that predatory birds, which need to manoeuvre quickly, have even higher rates. What is clear is that birds see far more detail in fast-moving events than we can. Like dragonflies, they would see the magic hidden in a shower of rain and, less poeti-cally but more practically, they can perceive the desperate manoeuvring of their prey as though it had been slowed down.

The need for high flicker-fusion rates becomes apparent when birds and insects are pitted against each other. Hobbies frequently hunt dragonflies and, although the acuity of vision of these small falcons is a hundred times that of the dragonfly, drag-onflies, in addition to perceiving smaller intervals of time, also have faster reaction

Opposite The time-expanding eyes of a hunter. Many predatory insects, such as this southern dragonfly, can see smaller intervals of time than we can. They could see the sculptured beauty of a water droplet (left), although at a much poorer resolution than that of human vision.

times. This combination makes the dragonfly formidable competition for a hobby hunting in the heat of the day. But the hobby has a simple solution. It waits. As the day cools down, so does the dragonfly, and this lowers both its flicker-fusion rate and its reaction time. Just before dusk, when the hobby hunts, the time battle has swung in the falcon's favour.

Time Confusion

Several snakes have discovered the advantages of outwitting the flicker-fusion frequency of their prey. Coral snakes in South America and the bandy-bandy in Australia both have highly coloured concentric rings around their bodies. In the past these were thought to act as warning colours, informing potential predators that the snakes were poisonous. However, as many hunters, such as laughing falcons and caracaras, successfully prey on other poisonous snakes, the real reason appears more complex.

As soon as the snake moves, animals with a low flicker-fusion rate, such as mammals, no longer see the concentric rings. The bands merge creating a brown blur that camouflages the snake against its background. The bold stripes become startlingly visible again as soon as the snake stops. The sudden change from camouflage to shock tactics seems to confuse attackers and allows a chance of escape.

Predators with a higher flicker-fusion rate, such as birds, experience a different optical illusion. Although they see the moving bands clearly, they may appear to travel backwards. A similar effect is sometimes seen in old westerns, when the film speed conflicts with the speed of rotation of a wagon wheel and creates strobing. This disconcerting apparent reversal of movement causes a predator to dive at the wrong end of the snake, allowing it to slink away unharmed.

Slow Time Worlds

Just as different predators have different perceptions of the snake's markings, so every animal has a slightly different perception of time. While some sense small intervals of time, others sense intervals too long for us to notice.

As we saw in Chapter 1, alligators call to each other with infrasonic sounds pitched at the lower limits of human hearing. Another alligator may wait 20 minutes before giving its reply. Such long-winded communication took a long time to be discovered, as we humans are not used to such slow time worlds. In the same way, some creatures see slow-moving objects that to us appear stationary.

Crabs can see the movement of the sun or moon across the sky — to them it appears as a moving blur. As it travels, it points west and crabs use this information for orientation. Both rabbits and dogs appear to see this movement too, so slow-motion detectors may also occur in other animals.

Mosquitoes have a low-resolution view of the world, not only in terms of visual acuity, but also because they simply cannot perceive rapidly moving objects. High-speed vision is simply unnecessary for mosquitoes, which live by sucking blood from slow-moving or sleeping creatures. The only downside is that they become easy prey for speedy predators such as dragonflies.

Warping Time

Although animals perceive different time worlds, their view is not necessarily constant; it might change depending on prevailing weather conditions.

We see because light focused by the lens in our eye reacts with light-sensitive chemicals, known as phytochemicals, in the cones and rods of the retina to give an impression of light, shade and colour. Because this is a chemical process, it is affected by temperature and the reactions take longer as the air cools. Warm-blooded animals, such as birds and mammals, maintain their vision even on the coldest days, but cold-blooded creatures need to stay warm if they are to perceive fast-moving events.

A garden tortoise, having survived the winter in hibernation, experiences a visual time warp the moment the lid is removed from its box of hay. Still cold and bleary-eyed, it blinks as light burns down on its retina for the first time in many months. Its eye's cold phytochemicals react slowly to the flood of sensory information. Gradually they start to resolve an image of the room, but the excited child, moving about above the tortoise, is never in one place long enough to register in any detail. The only trace the child's movements leave behind is a blurred smear. Only if she stops to peer at her pet does the smear resolve into a defined image but, as soon as she moves her hand to pick up the tortoise, she vanishes in a blur once more.

As the tortoise is carried into the garden, its disorientated vision continues – the world smudges past in a fog as though the tortoise were riding a helter-skelter with liquid walls. Only when it comes to rest on the grass does this molten world stabilize into a meaningful form. The streaming shapes above now solidify to form recognizable trees, the house no longer flows like lava and the surrounding grass is reassuringly stable. Even the child resolves momentarily as she stops to check the condition of her pet, although she would vanish into a streak again as soon as she ran away to play.

Such impaired vision might seem a handicap, but the world, observed at tortoise pace, appears reassuringly normal. The tortoise's slow-moving surroundings have plenty of time to register in the eye. Quick objects generally pose it few problems; even if they did, the tortoise is too sluggish to avoid them. It simply bides its time in its protective shell until danger passes.

Above and opposite When cold, a crocodile has slow reaction times, and its vision reacts slowly too. It needs to bask in the sun to stop fast-moving prey simply vanishing in a blur.

But the tortoise's time perception can change. As the sun heats its shell, strange things happen: smears on the landscape resolve into playing children and, when a ball rolls near, the tortoise sees it and retracts into its shell. Heat improves its visual time perception and lets it share our time world.

Because tortoises feed on stationary leaves, such temperature-dependent time perception has little effect on their eating habits, but for cold-blooded predators things are very different.

Before a crocodile can hunt it needs to sunbathe. Unlike warm-blooded predators, it has to heat up before it can even see its prey. When crocodiles bask on the riverbank, they are often inspected nervously by wildebeest or zebra, desperate for a drink. Providing the herd keeps moving and the crocodile is cold, the animals have nothing to fear — the crocodile sees them only as a blur. But as the reptile warms up, it starts to focus on its prey. Eventually even the fastest moving animals become visible. At this point the crocodile slinks back into the water and begins to stalk its victim.

Crocodiles are fortunate in that they inhabit hot climates where the sun usually provides the warmth they need in order to see and catch their prey. Cold-blooded predators living in a cold environment have a problem, but they solve it in an ingenious way.

Most sharks hunt initially by smell and hearing, then use an electric sense to home in on their prey. The notorious great white is different; in the final stages of the chase it is primarily a visual hunter. It even peeps out of the water surface to keep an eye on seals or other prey, a technique known as 'spy-hopping'. But as it patrols the chilly oceans rather than warm coral reefs, its eyes react too slowly to follow fast-moving prey. It has a clever but simple solution — eye heaters.

These work by shunting heat from the body's muscles into the eyes. By keeping its eyes warm, the shark is able to chase and catch even the fastest fish or seals. This device is so useful that other cold-water predators, such as swordfish, marlin and sailfish, all have their own designs.

Swordfish chase squid 600 metres below the surface where the water temperature may drop as low as 5°C. To penetrate the gloom, it has huge light-gathering eyes the size of grapefruits. But the swordfish has to maintain its image-intensifiers at temperatures of around $20{-}25^{\circ}$C if it is to tail-gate its prey at speeds of up to 60 kilometres an hour. Like sharks, swordfish solve their time-perception problem with a heat-producing organ that warms their brain and

eyes to well above the cold ocean temperature. When they finally catch the squid they rely on fast body actions to slash their prey in half with their rapier beaks.

Reaction Times

The speed of an animal's visual perception and the speed of its reaction times tend to move in step. Predatory animals need fast visual perception to follow their prey and quick reactions to catch them. In turn, prey animals need to see the predator coming and take even quicker evasive action.

A fly is one of the fastest performers, as well as perceiving smaller time intervals than us; it reacts to our clumsy attempts to kill it in under a hundredth of a second, five times faster than our usual reaction times. To catch a fly an animal needs to outwit the fly's visual perception, its reaction times and the ability of such a tiny body mass to accelerate at lightning speeds. To beat this bundle of kinetic energy, predators often resort to traps or lures, such as a spider's web, or they develop devices that outpace the fly's reaction times. A toad or chameleon uses an extendible tongue that, in the blink of an eye, can be shot out to capture a flying insect – they can move this part of their body faster than they could ever move themselves.

Other animals have devised even more ingenious devices to catch fast-moving prey. The frogfish has developed its own time-splitting trap that operates at speeds that almost defy belief. Camouflaged as colourful coral, these bizarre bulbous fish crawl around the reefs of the world on modified fins that act like front legs. Their dorsal fin is modified too, but in a way that helps them catch their fast-food meals. In some species the fin is sculpted to resemble the favourite fisherman's bait, a lugworm; other frogfish use designs based on a shrimp or a fish. The frogfish dangles this enticing lure over its mouth and any fish tempted by the offer suffers an extraordinary fate – it vanishes as if by magic.

The secret behind the disappearing trick is a mouth that, in an instant, can be extended to twelve times its normal size to reach out and suck in prey. Such sleight of mouth happens in just four thousandths of a second – a time period so short that other members of the shoal remain unaware of the loss of their neighbour and frequently share its fate.

Unsurprisingly, a snail has one of the slowest reaction times of any animal. Tap a snail on its head and after a short delay it disappears into its shell. But tap it four times in one second and it attempts to crawl on to the stick – it is simply unable to discern the intervals between the taps, so it believes it has met a solid object.

Except for a few small animals living life at a snail's pace, little creatures tend to react more quickly than larger ones. This is because it takes less time for messages to get around their nervous system. Tweak a dinosaur's tail and it really does take a long time for the signal to reach the brain. Smaller animals have shorter wiring, so messages get there sooner simply because they have less far to travel.

Body Clocks

Animals perceive time differently and react at different rates but they all mark its passage in the same way.

The world has a universal rhythm and it is twenty-four hours long. As the Earth rotates, the sun rises and sets, creating a daily pulse of light that impinges on almost every creature on Earth. This circadian cycle, as it is called, is so overwhelming that life has evolved to beat in tune with its rhythm. In fact, every cell in every plant and animal marks time to the same universal beat. These body clocks, often synchronized by a master clock, govern an organism's activity and control most of its body processes.

Our own body clock signals when we should expect a meal or when we should sleep, but it also times the release of hormones, lowers body temperature at night and controls a host of other hidden physiological processes. It can account for some surprising effects, causing heart attacks to be more common in the morning and asthma to be worse in the daylight hours. We become aware of its influence when air travel takes us across time zones, creating the body disruption we call jetlag.

Like us, animals and plants use their body clocks to ensure that they are active at the right time of day and that their bodies are physiologically prepared for the tasks they face.

A bee's body clock accurately times its arrival at flowers, allowing it to visit different plants at pre-set times of the day. In turn, the blooms are ready, using their own internal clocks to trigger the release of nectar or open petals in welcome. By dividing the day up between them, flowers avoid competing for the bees' attention.

In Africa, five different species of driver ants, which live alongside each other, also use their circadian rhythms to avoid competition. They work in shifts, one species going home as the next one starts work. Bees and birds use their circadian rhythm to help them navigate, marking the sun's passage across the sky. By knowing its expected position at different times of day, they can use it as a compass.

Remarkably, even organisms that live for less than a day still have a circadian rhythm to time their activity. Cyanobacteria, which divide in less than twenty-four hours, have a daily rhythm that enables each generation, just before sunrise, to produce enzymes that help with photosynthesis (the process that manufactures the organism's food). These body clocks are synchronized to the sun's cycle but, even away from the sun's influence, they still tick off the minutes and hours. Although the mole rat is effectively blind and lives underground, its body clock beats to the sun's rhythm and tells it when it is safe to go to the surface.

Body clocks run independently of the sun, but they still need to refer to it occasionally to keep the clocks on time. In vertebrates the pineal (see Chapter 2, page 67) performs this daily monitoring of the varying sunlight. In amphibians, reptiles and birds this organ senses the changes directly through the skin. Mammals, including humans, perceive them through the eyes and the information is then relayed to the pineal gland. The pineal gland keeps the body running to time by releasing the hormone melatonin at intervals determined by a master clock found in the brain.

Although most organisms have a synchronizing master clock, miniature clocks are found in most cells of the body and, gruesomely, even a severed limb continues to mark time and its ticking clocks can be reset by exposure to light.

Although the body clocks of animals kept in perpetual darkness continue to monitor time, eventually, without daily reference to the sun, their twenty-four-hour cycle starts to drift. In humans, the drift stabilizes at a new period of just under twenty-six hours; other animals drift to a cycle of their own. Such inaccuracy might seem like a design flaw, but over millions of years the sun cycle has changed in length and because the body clock is adjustable it has coped with the changes. Anyway, each day, the sun acts as a huge synchronizer and this daily pulse of light resets body clocks of all the billions of organisms on Earth.

Yearly Clocks

Just as there are clocks that time the days, many organisms have clocks that time the years. Although many temperate animals or plants sense the passing seasons by monitoring the changing day length, they may also have a yearly clock that controls their reproductive cycles. In the tropics, where day length hardly varies, such circannual clocks have special significance. Birds that overwinter in the tropics, such as the garden warbler, need a yearly clock to tell them when winter is over in their breeding grounds so that they can return home.

Because conditions in the tropics are less variable than in temperate zones, animals that stay there have less need to maintain a strict yearly cycle. The sooty tern, the brown booby and the lesser noddy tern use their internal clocks to create breeding cycles of their own, ranging from eight to ten months.

The most bizarre clocks must be those possessed by the periodic cicadas of North America. These spend many years underground as a larva sucking the sap from the roots of trees. Then simultaneously, on some mysterious signal, they all emerge from the earth to breed. Each species varies in the number of years it stays underground; some spend thirteen years, others seventeen, but it is always a prime number, a peculiarity that is thought to make it difficult for predators, which multiply using a doubling of numbers, to synchronize their populations to these periodic gluts.

Opposite Super-heated vision. The great white shark is a cold-water hunter. It uses eye-warmers to maintain its high-speed perception.

Scaling

Although all life relies on clocks to time its existence, how long an individual survives depends on the speed at which it lives its life. This speed is known as an animal's metabolic rate. It is measured through heartbeats, breathing rates and the speed at which the body burns reserves of fuel. As anyone who has run for a bus knows, these functions are interlinked – heart rate and breathing rate increase together proportionately.

The rate of living is governed by the size of the animal. Smaller animals live in the metabolic fast lane; larger ones tick over in the crawler lane. Compare an elephant to an elephant shrew: about the only thing they have in common is a long, flexible nose. The elephant shrew weighs just a few grams; in one minute its heart buzzes 800 times and its lungs take around 200 breaths. Over the same period, a 5-tonne elephant's heart thumps twenty-five times and it takes just six slow breaths. In fact the elephant does everything around thirty times slower than the elephant shrew. They may share the same world, but for the two different creatures the same interval of time has a different meaning.

Similarly, a day for a mouse weighing 10 grams is equivalent to two months for a blue whale that weighs 100 tonnes. These different rates of living affect lifespan in the same way – small animals complete their lives faster than large ones. An elephant may live as long as 78 years, whales live at least 90–100 years, probably far longer, but a shrew or a mouse is lucky if it sees the year through. The longevity of most animals is directly related to their size, which in turn is linked to the rate at which they live. Generally all mammals, whether mouse, shrew or elephant, will each take around 200 million breaths and have 1000 million heartbeats in their lives.

Fortunately for us, humans have successfully increased their life expectancy over what it should be for our size. Other animals around our weight die at about 25–30 years. As if by confirmation, we use up our 1000 million heartbeats and 200 million breaths at around this time. Why are we such a fortunate exception?

Most wild animals die a violent death as food for others, but nature has a harsh way of dispensing with those that survive beyond their useful reproductive years. Animals, including humans, are built to self-destruct – ageing prevents wasting resources maintaining an unproductive body. But, as we evolved into increasingly intelligent and social creatures, the simple biological rule that declared us redundant once past breeding age no longer applied. People too old to have children still had a role in nurturing their offspring to adulthood or passing on their wisdom to others in the family group. The reverence afforded to old age in tribal societies confirms the value of stretching the biological rules governing ageing.

But nature's laws have only been extended, not repealed – like other animals, our metabolism still ticks away the years towards death.

Deadly Passion

The fact that most animals are built to self-destruct is demonstrated in an extraordinary way by an Australian marsupial mouse known as *Antechinus stuartii*. The males of this species are famed for their strange tendency to mate themselves to death. At the end of the winter, the hormones of *Antechinus* turn them into raging sex-maniacs. They are such enthusiastic Lotharios that one bout of love-making may last twelve hours. Once they finish one passionate session they immediately swap partners. Their marathon orgy may involve up to sixteen partners and for its duration they have no time to sleep, eat or drink. Not surprisingly, after several days of wild passion, they begin to show signs of fatigue. They look anorexic and haggard and they start to lose their hair. Rivals inflict further damage. As they lose condition their activities become dangerous – the marathon mating bout takes place in the tree-tops and, when the males collapse from exhaustion, they plummet to the ground like falling fruit, often expiring in the middle of a sexual act. Within two to three weeks all the males are dead. The corpses exhibit all the signs of severe degeneration – they are lean, wasted and heavily infected by parasites.

Although fortunately the message from *Antechinus* is not that indulging in frequent sex in bad for health, it does show that ageing can be initiated by hormones. Pacific salmon show similar catastrophic ageing after spawning. As they die, their rotting bodies enrich the spawning grounds, creating an algal bloom that nourishes their developing young.

Long Lifers

For most animals, ageing is dependent on the rate of living. Because of this there are various ways of prolonging life. One is to be cold-blooded, as the pace of life of cold-blooded creatures is affected by the surrounding temperature. When they are cold, their metabolism chugs along in slow motion, but as soon as they warm up it zips into fast-forward. The way in which this affects their longevity became apparent when the popular American sports fish, the wall-eye, was studied. In the hot southern states it survived just two to three years, but in the glacial-cold lakes of Canada the same species eked out twenty-five years of sluggish existence.

How long members of another group of cold-blooded creatures, the reptiles, can survive is often a matter of speculation, as the animals concerned outlive any single human observer. However, records in zoos and of family pets suggest that many live to great ages and that tortoises live the longest of all.

One giant Aldabran tortoise has an undisputed record of living for 152 years and many others of the species, such as those transported in the early nineteenth century to an island off Zanzibar, appear to be over 180 years old. Except for irrational

Given their huge difference in scale, what could elephants and elephant shrews (right) have in common besides a long flexible nose? They share the same number of heartbeats in their lives. Because of its high-speed living the elephant shrew uses its allocation thirty times quicker than the elephant.

Opposite above Giant tortoises, like this one from the Galapagos, are the longest lived of all vertebrates. Some can reach over 200 years of age.

Opposite below A slothful existence. Sloths exist in a state of perpetual slow motion – they spend 80 per cent of their time asleep and often nod off while feeding.

scientific scepticism, there is no reason to doubt that some of these huge lumbering creatures may top 200 years and could perhaps live as long as 250. A radiated tortoise, purportedly a gift from Captain Cook to the King of Tonga, is believed to have died at the age of 193. The secret of the tortoises' great antiquity is to live life slowly; even under extreme duress their top speed barely reaches 0.27 kilometres an hour and most of the time their metabolism exists on tick-over.

Taking life easy has been perfected by the tuatara, the New Zealand reptile whose ancestors walked the Earth among the dinosaurs. Its metabolic rate is just high enough to keep its vital body processes idling and it is so lethargic that it has been known to fall asleep while chewing its food. It is twenty years old before it reaches maturity and it then breeds only once every four years. Its idleness brings a reward of longevity – it can certainly look forward to around 100 years of life, possibly far longer and some speculate an upper limit of 200 years.

Some mammals, too, use indolence to extend their lives. Sloths, for example, live up to their name. They have a metabolic rate 40–45 per cent of that expected for an animal of their size and they live in a perpetual state of slow motion. They spend over 80 per cent of their lives asleep; when they are active, every movement is painfully deliberate. Even the process of eating a leaf appears to involve only the minimum exertion necessary. They need to conserve energy because the tropical leaves they eat provide little nourishment. Digestion is equally long-winded; it can take up to a month for food to pass from the stomach to the small intestine, a process which in a human takes just four hours.

Along with this depressed metabolism, sloths achieve the lowest body temperature of any active mammal. The two-toed sloth can drop its temperature to 24°C from a normal high of 33°C. All this slothfulness contributes to a long but inactive life. So could inactivity be the key to longevity?

Sell-by Dates

There are several theories of ageing, one recent idea suggesting that we are slowly being poisoned by the oxygen we breathe. Although this gas provides the energy that drives the processes of life, over time it also damages us by releasing rogue electrons from our cells which, when combined with atoms, create highly reactive and unstable 'free radicals'. These free radicals damage the molecules in our body and cumulatively cause us to age. As we have seen, animals that live their lives at a fast rate breathe faster and therefore age quicker.

Another compelling theory suggests that we age because the body is in a continual state of repair and renewal. After ten years almost every cell in our body has been replaced. But each repair is potentially imperfect; in this process of regeneration, mistakes and mutations happen. Over time, these mistakes become visible as the signs of ageing. Animals with faster metabolisms, whose body cells turn over more quickly, therefore age faster than animals with slow metabolisms.

Whatever the reason for ageing, it is apparent that animals living in the metabolic fast lane die sooner than those with a more leisurely existence. In the wild, animals avoid unnecessary activity, opting for a lazy existence whenever they can. Predators such as lions spend most of their days conserving their energy, hunting only when hungry and, even then, preferring to ambush prey rather than wasting energy chasing after it. They reserve their main burst of energy for the final charge. At this point the body is subjected to unavoidable physical stress. At every stride, shock waves travel up the leg, causing a judder that reverberates through the pounding creature. On average, a lion will endure five such damaging runs before it succeeds in catching its prey, and then the body faces even greater trauma. No animal readily gives up its life; a bucking zebra flails out with kicks, a wildebeest or buffalo hooks with its horns, so few lions can bring down their prey without suffering some jarring physical contact. These minor injuries soon heal, but they create wear and tear on the body that will need repair. Cumulatively, these imperfect repairs appear to speed the ageing process.

A wild lion is lucky to live 15 years, whereas a lion living an indolent life in a zoo may often reach 30. Similar increases in lifespan apply to almost all captive animals. Caged parrots can survive over 80 years; in the wild, they would be unlikely to live half that time. Cats, dogs and horses all show extensions to their natural spans.

Several factors affect these animals' survival in captivity. They are fed long after they would be too slow to catch food in the wild and as age causes them to slow down they are protected from predators. As a result, they age more slowly. Life in captivity has few pressures, even finding food requires little effort, and they are subjected to practically no physical environmental pressures, such as harsh weather or general wear and tear, at all. So the cycle of damage and repair is a fraction of what it would be in the wild. Their metabolism is also maintained at a low level, they hardly ever need to rev up the heart and consequently they live life with their systems permanently idling. They share our indolent world and profit from its comforts by living longer.

In the increasingly sophisticated and automated societies of the developed world we have effectively put ourselves into the same cocooned state of existence as our pets or captive animals. Shielded from environmental stresses we have slowed the ageing process and also avoided a premature and violent death. So if being lazy appears to extend life, should we indulge in the current mania for exercise that subjects our body to unnecessary physical trauma?

By helping maintain a good and efficient circulation, moderate exercise benefits health. Being physically fit also reduces resting heart rate and helps keep overall metabolism down. But people who take prolonged and extreme forms of exercise, such as professional athletes and marathon runners, are unlikely to be blessed with a long life. Their metabolic rate is kept at a continually high level and their heart-beats tick off the years at an inflated rate. More importantly, the daily stresses on their bodies soon take their toll on the immune system. In the short term, these people are more susceptible to minor infections; long term, they suffer sooner from the illnesses of old age, particularly those, such as osteoarthritis, associated with mechanical wear and tear. The continual cycle of injury and repair also causes damaged DNA and protein to accumulate and this helps contribute to ageing.

So if running the marathon is not the secret of a long life, what is? Generally it involves keeping reasonably active but reducing intense physical stress. Birds seem to have solved the problem by taking to the air.

As with mammals, the expected lifespan of a bird depends on its size – small garden birds live around five years; large birds such as albatrosses can live for 60. But these birds have a faster heart rate and a higher metabolism than mammals of a similar size, yet they live far longer. Why should this paradox exist? By flying it appears they escape the kind of damage that ground-living animals endure. They not only evade the regular impact of body against ground, they also effortlessly avoid dangerous encounters by taking flight. As if to confirm the rule, flightless birds have shorter lives than their winged counterparts and bats live several times longer than their ground-bound relatives, the shrews.

Creatures that live in water are also protected from the trauma that terrestrial animals encounter and they live correspondingly longer. Baikal seals have been recorded living for 56 years and Caspian seals for 50, at least twice the age of comparable land mammals. The bizarre sea cows, such as manatees and dugongs,

regularly live 50–60 years and one dugong survived to 73 years. The sea cows gain extra years by combining an aquatic life with a lowered metabolism.

Without wings or flippers, we have done well in the ageing stakes, but our lives are nothing compared to some organisms on Earth. They stride the millennia as though they were just passing decades.

Serial Longevity

Corals and the colonial sea anemones known as bryozoans are the oldest living animals. In theory, they live forever; in reality, the environment will always change to curtail their eternal lives. Even so, many exist for thousands of years. The secret to their immortality is the ability to bud off a succession of individuals known as polyps. These create branching structures reminiscent of the branches of trees. Whether these serial organisms can be considered a single individual is debatable, but they are as individual as the trees they resemble.

Lions reserve their energies for the final charge at their prey. At this point the body is subjected to extreme stress. Accumulatively, this may speed the ageing process.

Some trees live for similar periods of time. The bristlecone pines of North America are among the oldest, believed to date back 5500 years. The giant redwoods also span millennia and some have survived over 6000 years. The prize goes to a tree in the Prairie Creek Redwoods State Park in California, which is thought to be 12,000 years old. It is now 72.5 metres high with a diameter of nearly 6 metres. It was a seedling while Britain was still covered with ice from the last ice age.

Even though the last ice age acted like a bulldozer over Britain, scraping the land free of all plant life, ancient trees survive. The oldest is the Fortingall yew, growing in decrepit old age near Aberfeldy in Tayside, Scotland. As a seedling it first thrust upwards towards the light 4200 years ago.

The secret of the longevity of both trees and colonial animals is that they evolve as they grow. Trees grow from points of cell division known as meristems; a large oak may have up to 100,000 of these growth points and each meristem can show mutations that make it genetically distinct from its parent. A single tree consists of many branches, each slightly different from its neighbours. By evolving as it grows a tree competes against the thousands of generations of insect predators that try to out-evolve it.

Plants have another way of outwitting the relentless march of time. They can produce the time capsules known as seeds. Although those of the willow live only a few days without germinating, others, such as the oriental lotus or the alpine lupin, can leapfrog the millennia, surviving in a viable state for 3000 years or more.

Human Time Suspension

Our method of opting out of periods of time may not be impressive, but it every bit as mysterious. In our hunter-gathering past, nocturnal predators patrolled the night making it a dangerous time to be active. Like other diurnal animals, we kept out of trouble by synchronizing our sleep cycle to this hazardous period and, except for night-clubbers and party-goers, we generally maintain the same activity patterns today.

Sleep helps us survive in other ways too; by dropping heart and breathing rates, it allows the body to conserve energy. Predators are the kings of the couch potatoes, becoming active only when hungry, then lying back to digest their meal over several days. Lions and domestic cats sleep for a soporific 16 hours each day, so that a domestic cat that lives 12 years will actually have spent only four years awake.

Koalas are even dozier, slumbering for 18 hours or more a day. They subsist on an unnutritious diet of eucalyptus leaves and, by nodding off frequently, they conserve energy. Of all mammals, the opossum holds the record, snoozing away 20 hours of every day.

Because small animals have a higher metabolic rate than larger animals they gain more from taking it easy. Consequently, large animals doze for far less time; a good night's sleep for an elephant is as little as four hours and a giraffe makes do with a miserly two hours.

Dolphins have a strange kind of sleep; to avoid drowning they need to remain alert enough to return periodically to the surface of the water, so each side of the brain takes it in turns to sleep. Other marine mammals, including whales and seals, also employ this cerebral shift work.

Like most animals, we indulge in two kinds of sleep: quiet sleep in which there is little brain activity, and active sleep, characterized by rapid eye movements and high brain activity. The periods of active sleep are when we dream.

Dreaming has always been linked to the SuperNatural. This is the time when the mind seems to be free-running and our ancestors believed that we contacted the spirits of the dead or entered different states of being. There appears something primal about dreaming that modern science can only confirm; it originates in the evolutionary oldest part of our brains – known as the reptile brain because of its links to the brains of prehistoric animals. Far from being a singularly human characteristic, dreaming is so ancient that *Tyrannosaurus rex* probably dreamed of hunting dinosaurs. It now seems fundamental to almost all higher animals.

A cat alternates 30-minute bouts of light sleep with six or seven minutes of deep sleep in which it twitches its ears, paws and tail and often mutters and growls. It also shows the rapid eye movements that signify dreaming. We can only guess at the contents of its dreams, but birds and mice are likely to be favourite subjects. Similarly, its prey probably has nightmares of being chased by cats. Opossums sometimes show running limb movements while asleep which suggest that they are having just these kinds of unsettling dreams.

Because sleep arose so early in evolution, it must have deep significance for all higher forms of life. It seems to provide many benefits; infants and children spend more time dreaming than adults and even the unborn show dream-type brain activity, which implies that dreaming stimulates the brain over the crucial period of early development. Each night, it seems to have a role sifting and cataloguing new experiences gained through the day. This nightly inventory probably continues in adults and helps commit to memory the significance of the day's events.

Lions spend 16 hours a day asleep. They probably dream of catching zebra.

Some people believe that dreaming also prepares an animal for the activities it encounters in life. Without any danger or risk of failure, a cat can mentally run through confrontations with rivals or follow the motions of catching a mouse, readying it for the times these activities are needed. In the same way, prey animals can mentally rehearse their escapes without any risk.

Torpor

Whatever its other benefits, dreaming constructively utilizes many of the hours that animals spend each day asleep. Some animals opt out of the world for longer periods of time.

Hummingbirds have the highest metabolic rate of any vertebrate. Although, when perched, their heart rate is similar to that of other small birds, ticking away at 700–850 beats per minute, as soon as they begin to hover it buzzes up to an awesome 1200 beats per minute. They use more fuel for their size than a jet fighter.

If we lived our lives at the same pace as a hummingbird, we would have to consume forty-five 1-kilo bags of sugar a day just to stay active.

If we were to expend energy at this rate our body temperature would rise to nearly 400°C and we would need to consume forty-five 1-kilogram bags of sugar per day. But hummingbirds can live 12 to 15 years, several times longer than other birds of an equivalent size. How do they do it?

At times hummingbirds drop their body temperature from an active 38–42°C to below 13°C – and simultaneously slow their metabolism drastically. In this state of torpor, with their feathers fluffed up and their beak pointing skywards, their heart rate may drop to a twentieth of its norm, as low as 50 beats per minute. Although their metabolic rate is now equivalent to the energy we expend watching television, they are effectively dead to the world. They use torpor to conserve energy and opt out of unfavourable periods of time. Bats share this ability to cut down energy demands over difficult spells and they frequently allow their body temperature to drop during inactivity. Pocket mice also enter torpor when food is hard to find.

Torpor is usually a means of escaping cold weather, but the frilled lizard of the tropical regions of Australia uses it to avoid the heat. In the dry season, when food is short and the air temperature is high, it reduces its metabolism by 70 per cent and its body temperature by 5°C, thereby conserving energy throughout the arid spell. It often remains in the same tree for three months, moving slowly to stay in the shade and venturing to the forest floor once a week to feed on harvester termites. Despite its reduced metabolism it can still generate sudden bursts of energy to escape predators.

The dormouse is a true hibernator – able to drop its body temperature close to that of the surrounding air. It uses this state of time suspension to opt out of the unfavourable winter months.

Winter Sleep

Similar to torpor is the winter sleep of many animals. Winter is the least productive time of the year, food is scarce and the weather is inclement. Many animals, such as brown and polar bears, sleep through the winter inside a den that protects them from the harsh world outside. In this way American black bears snooze away seven months of the Canadian winter. This is no ordinary sleep – the bears' heartbeat drops appreciably, their breathing becomes shallow and they may last a month without turning over. However, their body temperature is kept only slightly below normal and, if disturbed, they can wake in an instant. Racoons and badgers also show this kind of deep winter sleep.

But other animals allow their body temperature to fall close to that of the surrounding air. These are the true hibernators.

Only small mammals truly hibernate, but animals as diverse as woodchucks, koalas, hamsters, hedgehogs and bats all use this technique. Arctic ground squirrels living in Alaska may hibernate for nine months of the year, as does the hoary marmot of North America and Siberia. Although its temperature drops, the animal retains control, setting its internal thermostat to the minimum needed to sustain life. For some animals this can be as low as 2°C.

That famous sleepyhead, the dormouse, has recently revealed a few surprises in its hibernation technique. Contrary to previous belief, instead of spending the winter in a tree hollow, most simply curl up in the leaf litter of a forest floor. Being exposed to the elements keeps them cooler and less likely to wake up at the wrong time. Even so, they have to stir themselves once a week to get rid of metabolic waste products.

Only one bird is known to hibernate – a type of nightjar known as the poorwill, which lives in the mountains of the Colorado Desert and passes the winter in a sheltered rock crevice. Here its heart and breathing rates drop to almost zero and its body temperature falls from a norm of 41°C to a low of 6°C. In this state of suspended animation, five hazardous winter months, when insects are hard to find, disappear in an instant.

These animals fulfil the human dream of taking a step into the future by putting themselves into a state of suspended animation. Others have discovered even more long-term techniques.

Cryogenics

Freezing living bodies has many problems. As temperatures approach freezing, water molecules in the body lock together creating a razor-edged lattice-work of ice molecules. As the icy structure grows, it jabs and slices the surrounding cell membranes, dicing them into fragments.

Animals that operate at low temperatures use the biological equivalent of antifreeze to lower the freezing point of the blood. Antarctic fish have a sugar protein in their blood that keeps it flowing while the surrounding water is freezing. But some animals take their bodies to even lower temperatures. These are the masters of cryogenics.

The painted turtle of North America is the most northerly occurring turtle. Adults hibernate at the bottom of lakes, under ice, where they become totally immobile. They stop breathing oxygen and their heartbeat drops so low it beats only once every ten minutes. They have even been shown experimentally to be resistant to poisons such as cyanide. Although the adults avoid becoming frozen, their offspring, which hatch in shallow burrows in the fall, regularly endure this icy fate. Rather than emerge to face a frozen wasteland, the hatchlings sit out the winter underground. Gradually the ice penetrates to them. Ice forms first in the blood, then it surrounds the internal organs, until eventually half the tiny turtle's total body water has turned to ice.

The secret of the turtle's ability to survive lies in the high concentrations of glucose, glycerol and taurine, an amino acid it stores in its body. These chemicals prevent the tissues shrinking. The glucose is also used as a fuel to maintain the body without oxygen. In the spring the hatchlings thaw out, their heartbeat resumes and they start to breathe again.

Wood frogs, grey tree frogs and the spring peeper of North America all use a similar technique to survive freezing. They pass the winter at the soil surface, covered by a loose layer of leaf litter that affords little protection from the cold blast of winter, which is often at an icy -8°C. Their blood contains protein molecules that actually encourage ice to form. Because there are millions of these ice-forming sites, no single crystal ever grows big enough to cause damage. As they form, they suck water out of the tissues. To compensate for this water loss, the frog's liver becomes a sugar factory, turning out glucose which circulates around its body. This syrup suffuses through the tissues, preventing the vital organs freezing. Because of this technique, the frog can be 65 per cent ice and still survive. In this state its breathing and heartbeat cease completely. When the time comes, it thaws from the inside out, freeing the heart to pump oxygen before the whole body has defrosted.

In the Arctic wastes of Russia, the Siberian salamander performs similar feats. The hard permafrost prevents it burrowing down to escape the cold. Temperatures may drop as low as -56°C, causing the salamander to become frozen among the surface soil and water.

Ice Microbes

Occasionally, in this tundra area, frozen relics of a previous age are dug up. Although largely intact, these mammoths could never be revived, but remarkably they may contain life that can.

Both bacteria and yeast, found among the mammoth's remains, can be revived thousands of years after they were originally entombed. However, this suspended animation is relatively short compared with microbes that have been extracted from Arctic ice probes. In Siberia in the 1980s bacteria were extracted from tens of metres down in permafrost that had been at -10°C for over three million years. As soon as they were brought out of the natural deep freeze they started to divide as though the thousands of millennia had never passed. Such microbes must frequently be revived naturally as glaciers melt.

The film *Jurassic Park* was based on the premise that mosquitoes, trapped in amber, contained DNA from the blood of dinosaurs and, from this genetic blueprint, the terrifying animals could be resurrected. The practicality of such a project has generated considerable scientific scepticism, but recently a scientist in California has achieved something almost as remarkable – he appears to have revived living organisms from amber that is 30 million years old. These prehistoric creatures were hardly on the scale of dinosaurs – in fact they were invisible to the human eye – but they represented extinct forms of life. They were found resting as dormant spores among trapped soil particles. The most intriguing were a variety of *Staphylococcus* bacteria that differed from today's bacteria in the nature of the fatty acids found in their cell walls. Such micro-dinosaurs are the world's greatest time-travellers.

Just as animals live in different time worlds depending on the needs of their existence, so each responds in different ways to the forces that impinge on Earth. Although we are largely unaware of these hidden and mysterious powers, they deeply affect the life that surrounds us and their influence extends even to our own lives. These forces are the subject of the final chapter of this book.

A fly preserved in amber, a fossilized tree sap. Scientists have revived organisms that have been trapped in amber for over 30 million years.

6

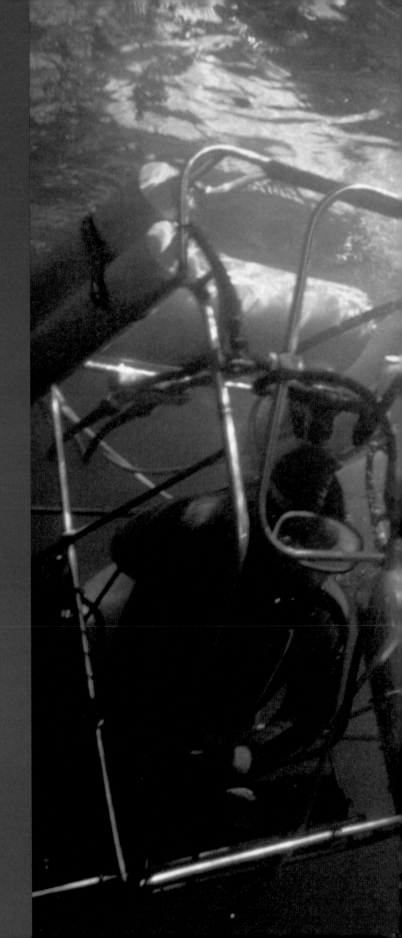

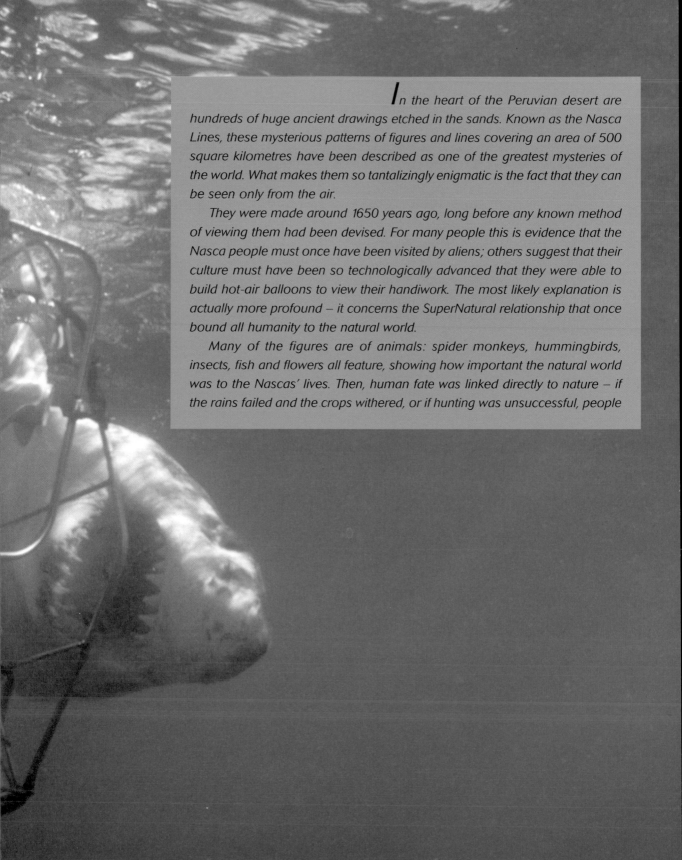

In the heart of the Peruvian desert are hundreds of huge ancient drawings etched in the sands. Known as the Nasca Lines, these mysterious patterns of figures and lines covering an area of 500 square kilometres have been described as one of the greatest mysteries of the world. What makes them so tantalizingly enigmatic is the fact that they can be seen only from the air.

They were made around 1650 years ago, long before any known method of viewing them had been devised. For many people this is evidence that the Nasca people must once have been visited by aliens; others suggest that their culture must have been so technologically advanced that they were able to build hot-air balloons to view their handiwork. The most likely explanation is actually more profound – it concerns the SuperNatural relationship that once bound all humanity to the natural world.

Many of the figures are of animals: spider monkeys, hummingbirds, insects, fish and flowers all feature, showing how important the natural world was to the Nascas' lives. Then, human fate was linked directly to nature – if the rains failed and the crops withered, or if hunting was unsuccessful, people starved. Each tribe had its own human emissary to make contact with the forces that controlled the natural world. These spiritual go-betweens were known as shamans. To make their mind journeys shamans used drugs or relentless rhythmic drumming that sent them into an altered state of reality. In these out-of-body experiences they were able to look down from an apparently floating vantage point – a view that the Nasca Lines seem to satisfy. Such shamanic travelling is not accepted by modern science, but for the practitioners of the time it was a vital way to gain information about the world. When the Nasca Lines were drawn, the society was in crisis and the shaman's role had crucial significance: the climate was becoming drier and the shaman needed to summon the natural powers to bring rain to the parched land.

Shamans are used by all societies that depend directly on the natural world for their survival, from the Inuit in the Arctic to the Yanomami of the Amazon and the Bushmen of Southern Africa. Shamanism is a belief system that dates back into prehistory. Early shamans executed the cave paintings of animals, found in Lascaux in France and other prehistoric sites, as they tried to gain control over the animals they hunted. In the Kalahari in Africa, Bushmen drew similar paintings, a practice that stopped only at the beginning of the twentieth century. Intriguingly, some of the paintings show pictures that are half-man and half-animal, for in the trance state shamans sometimes took the ultimate step in contacting the natural world and believe that they became animals. Even today, Bushmen still believe that powerful shamans can turn into lions and acquire their animal powers.

To these peoples shamanism is a way of making sense of the natural world. They have no feeling of superiority over nature. Instead they recognize that they are part of it; their quest, through trance, is to become more closely

entwined with it. To acquire the power of an animal is the ultimate act of shamanic ritual.

In Europe, the old beliefs were continued by witches; they believed that their hallucinogenic potions gave them the ability to shape-shift, turning into ravens or other creatures. Their powers were once respected, and their herbal knowledge made them the general practitioners of the day. But, because they represented a rival religion to Christianity, they eventually became persecuted in witch-hunts and their rituals had to be practised in secret.

But people who held power over the natural world always had a role in society, and some seemed to have particular influence over animals. Among these specialists were the horse whisperers.

Horse Whispering

In the past, if a horse refused to submit to the process of domination involved in breaking its will, the horse whisperer was called upon to exercise his powers. This man belonged to an élite band who used bewitching powers to tame intractable animals. Included in the whisperer's magical armoury was the bone of a toad steeped in aromatic oils but, that apart, the whole operation seemed to involve the uttering of a single whispered word.

In the past, the horse whisperer was one of the most sought-after specialists in the farming communities of both Europe and North America, but because of a possible connection with witchcraft he was also treated with suspicion. Today, there are still practitioners of this art and they have given us an insight into what lay behind the ancient powers. It seems the horse whisperer had learned the secret language of horses.

Horses communicate mainly through body language. By mimicking the postures of a dominant horse the horse whisperer begins to gain control. This is possible because horses belong to a structured society. Whenever they move, the dominant mare takes the lead and the other horses, in order of rank, follow behind, the stallion taking the rear. This order is rigidly maintained and horses that fall out of line are immediately dealt with. Their punishment is to be excluded from the herd.

Like refusing a naughty child the attention it craves, this treatment is an effective form of discipline. But an ostracized animal is also vulnerable; denied the protection of the herd, his solitude can prove fatal. The delinquent horse soon becomes nervous and tries to rejoin the group. At first the stallion signals his indignation by staring and advancing menacingly, but once he decides the punishment is over he turns away and, through subtle changes of posture, signals that the contrite horse may rejoin the herd.

The horse whisperer mimics these movements and in turn reads the subtle cues given off by the horse. Like the stallion, he is skilled in the art of rejection, turning away from the horse and causing it to come forward when its natural reaction would be to flee. He deals with the horse using its own language, and the communication is swift and clear. Ultimately, the horse seeks human friendship willingly and quickly learns its position among people as it would in a natural herd.

Even among people who spend their whole lives with horses, few ever learn to 'speak' this secret language. In the modern world we have become physically and spiritually separated from nature – conscious communication with it is rare. However, we still send out signals to other organisms; we are simply unaware of their meaning. Among the messages that we unknowingly transmit are those given off by smell.

Opposite Bushmen painted these rock impressions of pink elephants. Some paintings show pictures that are half animal and half man, suggesting that Bushmen believed they could enter the animal world while in a state of trance.

On the Scent

For humans, the idea that body odour is offensive is a relatively recent concept. Although we are largely hairless, the tufts that still grow under our armpits or in our pubic regions are actually scent traps, acting as a biological reserve for the bacteria that break down our skin secretions and create our natural scent. No matter how we scrub these areas clean, our pets are only too aware of our odours. A dog can identify an individual by scent alone and tracker dogs are even able to distinguish the smells of identical twins. Some of our odours give out unintended signals. The skin folds and creases between our toes are home to PABA (para amino bezoic acid), a pheromone closely related to the vaginal odours of a bitch on heat. It is perhaps no surprise that dogs show such exuberant enthusiasm for these areas.

Cats react differently to our odours – they do their best to disguise them. When a cat rubs itself against our legs, it transfers odour from its cheek glands to us, merging its own smell with ours and making us appear part of its family.

Chemicals that influence the behaviour of animals are called pheromones. Often they cause a sexual response. These secret signals are so pivotal to the lives of other mammals that it would be surprising if human beings were an exception. Indeed, various studies show that pheromones have a considerable influence on us. When photographs of women were sprayed with the scent chemical androsterone, men rated them more highly in attractiveness than those that had not been sprayed. The same chemical smeared on the upper lips of woman had an aphrodisiac effect. A chair in a dentist's waiting room, laced with androsterone, attracted more women to sit on it than men.

We share this chemical signalling with pigs. Vets use a commercial equivalent of androsterone, known as 'Boarmate', to put a sow in the mood for mating. In nature she would respond to the androsterone in the saliva of the amorous male. Because the valuable truffle exudes a chemical that mimics androsterone, French farmers sometimes use female pigs to sniff out this fungus from deep underground. The truffle's sexual scent may also account for its famed aphrodisiac qualities among gourmets.

All these facts point to pheromones having the same kind of subsconcious influence on us as they do on other animals. But strangely, although these secret signals generally enhance our attractiveness, we do our best do rid ourselves of them. Ironically, we blast them away with the sexual scent secretions of other animals. The most sophisticated and expensive perfumes

Opposite A full body suit of bees. This strange attire is made possible by harnessing the controlling pheromone of the queen bee. The tube helps the man breathe through the swarm.

Below When it stings, the killer bee pumps out a pheromone which incites other bees to join the attack.

contain musk from the ventral pouches of the musk deer, castoreum from beavers' anal glands or extracts from the anal sacs of civet cats. Cheaper perfumes make do with synthesized versions of these smells.

If we are not using the secret sexual signals of animals, we use the chemical messages of plants instead. A fragrant chemical known as methyl jasminate is a major ingredient in most cologne. While we use it to enhance our attractiveness, some plants use it to convey a different message. When insects attack, the damaged leaves release methyl jasminate as a message for the plant to increase its chemical defences. The plant kingdom has a witch's brew of literally thousands of toxic chemicals in its arsenal. The chosen poison of the tobacco plant, for example, is the addictive nicotine found in cigarettes; as little as a day after an attack, this can reach lethal levels up to 600 times higher than normal. All this chemical warfare is triggered by methyl jasminate.

Every time we pass near a plant our perfumes are sending out hidden signals, telling the plant it is under attack. It starts increasing its chemical protection and, although this might seem like good news for the plant, the stress of producing poisons actually weakens it. So we are slowly killing the plants with scent. Because of this, in some laboratories studying the growth of plants, women – and men – are banned from wearing perfume in case it sends out the wrong message.

Killer Bees

Our appreciation of the scent of flowers is a useful by-product of the chemical signals plants give off in order to attract insects for pollination. Among these pollinators are bees, whose world is totally governed by smell. Ignorance of the complexity of their smell world has had devastating consequences.

In São Paolo, Brazil, in 1957, a breeding experiment went terrifyingly wrong; in a quest to breed the perfect bee, the docile European honey-bee was crossed with the aggressive but highly productive African bee. Instead of creating docile and productive offspring, the hybrid inherited the deadly ferocity of its African parent. In classic horror-movie fashion, it escaped from the research station and, possessing the African bees' migratory nature, headed up towards North America.

Bees defend their hive to the death. Guard bees, at the entrance, act as bouncers, security-checking visitors. They react to gate-crashers by extending their stings and wafting out a fruity aroma. This pheromone drives the hive into a frenzy and the bees pour out in a drunken fury. Killer bees differ from honey-bees only in that their fuse is shorter; once they are aroused, nothing placates them. They are the yobs of the insect world. Even the vibrations of passing tractors or lawnmowers can incense them and send them streaming out of the hive looking for trouble.

True to their olfactory nature they home in on smell. They find the carbon dioxide of breath particularly aggravating and, unfortunately for us, hairsprays and perfumes create a super-aggressive signal. The first bee to sting is on a kamikaze mission, but its death will have served the good of the hive. As the impaled barb pulls away from the bee's body, it continues to pump venom, simultaneously releasing an alarm pheromone. When the scrambled swarm receive the signal they fly in to attack.

If you are attacked by killer bees, trying to escape by jumping in a pond or river is futile. They may wait for two hours or more for you to reappear. The only effective defence is to run. But you need to be fit; although a fast runner can outrun a flying bee, the killer variety are so persistent they may follow for up to 1.5 kilometres. But there is little alternative; killer bees can remain in a deadly state of arousal for as much as a week. They are still a problem in some of the southern states of America, but dilution with less virulent strains has taken some of the sting out of their advance.

Ignorance of the bee's secret language of scent can create problems for humans. But there are some beekeepers who are so in tune with their charges that they can coat themselves with bees to create 'bee beards' or, in some extreme cases, full body suits of living bees. These people often surface from the experience with barely a sting. Their secret? A scent formula based on the pheromone the queen bee uses to subdue the hive.

Death Traps

When we understand the secret language of insects we can turn it to our advantage. For example, the fluorescent flytraps that hum on the walls of many food shops are tuned in to the hidden ultraviolet signals that insects use. They emit an enticing blaze of ultraviolet light, invisible to the human eye, that lures the insects to death by electrocution; this glow simulates the patch of skylight that, in nature, guides insects out of dense vegetation. Inevitably, nature came up with the idea first.

Spiders such as the American *Hexurella* and *Hypochilus* species incorporate sheets of ultraviolet silk in their webs that, to the fly, look like glistening escape routes. The flies are trapped as they make their getaway. Some spiders have refined this basic design by constructing an inconspicuous web beneath the ultraviolet lure to catch any escapees. There are even spiders that entice insects directly with an abdomen glowing with reflected ultraviolet light.

Some spiders attempt a different approach, weaving into their webs ultraviolet designs that mimic the honey guides of flowers. This deadly subterfuge has many variations. Insectivorous plants, including the Venus flytrap and the pitcher plant, have discovered the same trick and incorporate ultraviolet markings in their designs to ensure a steady stream of prey.

Opposite Hatchling turtles make their way towards the glow of the horizon; their sense of direction can easily become confused by the lights of beachside hotels.

Right Death traps. Like the exterminating machines used in butchers' shops, the Venus flytrap uses ultraviolet lures to attract flies into its deadly embrace.

Trick of the Light

Although we consciously manipulate invisible ultraviolet to cause confusion to insects, light emitted in the wavelengths we can see creates even greater natural bewilderment.

When hatchling turtles make their way to the sea at night, they use the glow of light, still dying on the horizon, to help guide them to the water. Near some turtle beaches the light-spill from newly built tourist hotels can cause the animals to become disorientated – they may end up among the diners instead of in the sea. Flying around the lights are insects in a similar state of confusion.

Moths have a simple method of navigation that served them well for millions of years. As they fly they keep the moon in the same position in the sky relative to their body. This helps them maintain a straight-line course. Or at least it did until we created artificial moons in the form of electric lights. When the moth tries the same trick with these lights it simply ends up spiralling into them.

Birds face the same problems. They also seem to use the moon as a means of orientating and consequently, when flying over open water at night they sometimes mistake a lighthouse beacon for the moon. In storms when the clouds obscure the night sky, birds crash-land at lighthouses in their hundreds.

Our lights can cause other problems too. On clear nights birds navigate by the stars, but when migrants traverse North America they are faced with a strange phenomenon. In places the star fields appear inverted, spread across the ground instead of in the sky. These twinkling cityscapes present a confusing and deadly signal to the migrating birds. As they try to interpret the strange guiding lights they are drawn ever closer. Each year 100 million birds collide with city skyscrapers. The Sears Tower in Chicago, the tallest skyscraper in the United States, kills 1500 alone and 10,000 a year die in Toronto's financial district. In some places building lights are deliberately switched off over the migration period in an attempt to save avian lives.

In Toronto the migrants face a new hazard. Like shipwreckers of old, luring hapless ships on to unseen rocks, city gulls harry the birds towards the glowing buildings. These town pirates have learned the routes through the maze of lights and reflective glass and manoeuvre expertly through the dangers. The gulls began their marauding lives by feeding on the casualties, but in time they learned their own ways of increasing the death toll.

Fire Traps

Light, deeper than any red we can see, causes confusion of a different kind for some insects. As we saw in Chapter 4, the fire beetle *Melanophila* is tuned into the narrow band of infrared radiation given off by fire and it uses this hidden signal to find freshly charred wood in which to lay its eggs. The message from a forest fire may reach the beetles from 50 kilometres away.

The beetles developed this remarkable sense long before early humans had mastered fire. Nowadays the system is easily confused. Swarms of beetles, attracted by the massed thermal radiation from thousands of cigarettes, have been known to descend on football matches. In their quest for fire, they also frequently turn up at barbecues, sugar refineries and smelting plants.

Electric Messages

Fire was one of mankind's first discoveries, but the most confusing secret messages are emitted by our more recent inventions.

Electricity now pervades every home and is carried across the countryside on huge pylons. Around every wire is a force field of electromagnetism that radiates out into the environment. Recently these forces have been implicated in promoting leukaemia in people living close to high-voltage powerlines and in America, because of the potential dangers, no new houses are to be sited under lines. As revealed in Chapter 3, bees seem to be only too aware of the danger and will swarm from any hive placed under the lines. Birds also avoid flying near or perching on them, and small mammals will not choose to nest near any high-voltage source.

But electric fields can have positive effects as well. Surprisingly, plants appear to like electricity and there have been consistent reports that they grow better under pylons. In experiments, plants subjected to high-intensity electromagnetic fields grow up to twice as fast as normal. The electricity is believed to help calcium ions flow through the cells. Calcium stimulates the enzymes that cause growth; the result is more luxuriant foliage.

This promotion of plant growth has also been seen near the antennae of the US Navy's Project Seafarer in Wisconsin and Michigan. These transmitters use low-frequency electromagnetic waves to broadcast messages to submarines anywhere in the world. Each of the five facilities consists of a transmitter connected to long overhead wires that stretch for 100 kilometres across the countryside.

Since the antennae were switched on in 1986 the trunks of aspens and red maples under the antennae have grown thicker and red pines have grown taller than their neighbours away from the transmitters. Bathed in the electromagnetic field, moss also appears to grow more luxuriantly. Again it seems likely that calcium ions, helped by the field, were responsible for the surge in growth.

Among other strange effects was the reaction of young deer mice to these electromagnetic fields. They too seemed to grow faster, opening their eyes earlier than mice away from the field did. It seemed that in some way the electromagnetic field increased their metabolic rate. Leaf-cutter bees experienced less positive effects, surviving the winter less well than those that lived away from the antennae.

Artificial star-fields
created by city lights.
Migrating birds
(opposite) can
become confused
by the apparent
inversion of the night
sky caused by city
lights and, as a result,
may crash-land into
high-rise buildings.

There was also a surprising effect on migrating birds; when the antennae were switched on, the migrants, studied on radar, seemed to deviate from their normal course. No doubt the transmissions interfered with their magnetic sense.

Project Seafarer was set up to communicate with submarines, but these were already creating their own confusion in the oceans. The submarines tow a long hydrophone rod (an apparatus for listening to sounds conveyed under water) in order to eavesdrop on enemy subs. The electronics inside the equipment create their own array of electric fields and these attract hammerheads and other sharks which have been known to sever the cable, no doubt mistaking it for food.

Electric Confusion

Until humans came on to the aquatic scene, everything electrical in the ocean was potential prey for the sharks. But our recent harnessing of electricity can cause great confusion. Sharks will attack divers' flashguns or any electrical items such as battery-driven radios or torches that might fall into the water. They also have a fascination with metal objects. When bottom-feeders such as tiger sharks are caught and cut open they often disgorge an assortment of metal garbage ranging from tin cans to rusty number plates. Although not electrical in themselves, some metals react with salt water to produce an electric current strong enough to simulate the signals of their prey. The metal hulls of boats are sometimes attacked for just this reason.

Sharks have also been known to sever communication cables, attracted by the electricity that flows through them. Often the only clues to what caused the break were shark teeth impaled in the frayed ends of the cable. As each repair cost around $250,000, the wire companies soon redesigned their cables with screening to prevent electricity leaking into the water.

Sonic Overhead

Our technological world creates many sounds we cannot hear and these affect animals — and humans — in mysterious ways. Traffic generates the low-frequency sounds known as infrasound (see Chapter 1) and underground gas pipes, air-conditioning systems and aircraft all contribute to this subsonic din. These sounds, pitched below human hearing, may have an invidious effect on our general health.

The infrasound that hums around some offices from air-conditioning systems contributes to the general malaise known as sick-building syndrome. This effect happens because certain critical frequencies set our own organs into resonance. The military have no doubt about the destructive power of infrasound and have designed and tested sonic weapons that maim or kill by causing the internal organs to resonate catastrophically.

In the animal world infrasound is used as a long-distance communication system, so we can only guess at some of the confusion that our artificial sources of infrasound create. In Florida, in the breeding season, male alligators bellow out their dominance by calling across the swamps in infrasound, as we saw in Chapter 1. Recently they have had to face unfair competition. Airboats, used to cross the swamps, emit a barrage of infrasound from their huge air-churning propellers. The reptiles take this as a direct challenge to their manhood and respond by arching their backs in classic bellowing pose and making as much infrasonic noise as they can. But overwhelming competition comes each time a space shuttle blasts into space from the Kennedy Space Centre. Then, infrasonic waves reach every male alligator in Florida, defying them to enter a duel of sound. The alligators respond gamely, but it is a battle they can never win.

Human-created infrasound sometimes travels around the world. In 1996, when the French tested their nuclear arsenal with an underground explosion on Muraroa Atoll in the Pacific, the infrasonic waves from the blast radiated across the world at the speed of sound. Eleven and a half hours later every street pigeon in Paris would have heard them. The birds may have even let off an infrasonic alarm call as a hidden protest.

Ocean Soundings

Sonic pollution has even greater influence in the oceans of the world. Humans now fill the seas with a cacophony of noise. The low-frequency throb of tankers and heavy container ships penetrates far into the ocean and, over the last 30 years, background noise levels have increased tenfold in the busier shipping lanes.

So how does all this racket affect ocean life? Whales are the most sound-sensitive organisms in the oceans. The low-frequency calls of the baleen whales, such as the fin and blue, span oceans at the quietest part of the natural ocean sound spectrum – below the interference from the majority of other ocean sounds, but above the infrasonic rumbling of earthquakes. Unfortunately for the whales, today's human-produced sounds transmit in the very same frequencies chosen for the whale's secret sound channel. We are effectively jamming their calls and this must be hampering the whales' ability to communicate long distance.

Underwater drilling rigs off Newfoundland create a bewilderment of noise which humpbacks will make a detour to avoid; around these rigs the whales appear more likely to blunder into fishing nets.

The military add more noise pollution. They use a low-frequency active sonar system that creates a thunderous 235 decibels of sound to track submarines. It works by sending pulses of high-intensity, low-frequency sound into the ocean and

listening for the echoes that bounce off submarines. When these sonic divices were tested on migrating grey whales off the coast of California, the whales made huge detours to avoid them. Mothers with calves reacted with the same defensive behaviour used against killer whales – they swam close to the shore and their calves hugged the side of the body away from the open ocean. Considering this proven disturbance, it was probably no coincidence that when a NATO vessel conducted low-frequency sonic tests in the Kyparrisiakos Gulf in the Ionian Sea, twelve Cuvier's beaked whales stranded themselves on a local beach.

Whale Rescues

Throughout history most strandings have happened without our confusing signals adding to the whales' navigational errors. The difference today is the reception that now awaits the whales on the beach.

In our ever-changing relationship with the natural world, one of the most significant developments has been in our attitude towards the largest mammals on earth. Once hunted to the point of near extinction, they have now become one of the most valued of all creatures. When a whale's navigation sense goes awry and a pod strands itself on a beach (see Chapter 3, page 84), hundreds of people arrive to attempt a rescue. Considerable human effort and cost is directed at returning the whales to the sea.

Part of this change of attitude has arisen because the discoveries of science have revealed just how remarkable the powers of these animals are. They are now something that excites wonder. People not only feel the need to rescue them; many join whale-watching tours where the cetaceans become a focus of pilgrimage. The key to this fascination is the fact that, although they appear alien, whales are not only intelligent, they also appear to possess mysterious powers that are, in some ways, borne out by science.

Whales have the most sophisticated sound-imaging system in the world. The techniques they use are now being copied by science as they try to develop under-sea exploration that can operate in murky water. Recently, humpback whales have been discovered to work as a team, corralling fish by creating an enveloping wall of bubbles. It also seems that killer whales can stun fish by slapping their tails against the surface of the ocean.

The list of whales' powers seems endless and, almost monthly, remarkable new discoveries are being made. The haunting song of the humpback is now a familiar

sound to many people, but it has always been assumed that humpbacks, unlike the fin and the blue whale, do not call with long-distance infrasound. Recent research has overturned this assumption. Even the song, which is the most complex in the animal world, continually turns up new surprises. Although the whales maintain the same themes through each breeding season, they add flourishes and variations just as humans might improvise around a tune. Like us, they also employ rhymes, a technique that we use to help us remember complex songs. Even though whales and humans diverged in evolution about 60 million years ago, our brains still retain enough similarities to share the same singing techniques. Perhaps our new-found affinity for these creatures should not surprise.

Pet Power

The animals to which we feel closest are those that, like whales, have a social aspect to their lives. Some of these we have chosen as our pets. As our lives entwine we occasionally gain glimpses of their hidden powers.

Many of us share our lives with either a dog or a cat. Of the two, the cat has changed less through the process of domestication and in outward looks and behaviour it is almost identical to the wild cat. The dog now appears in motley guises, but behaviourally, beneath the skin, it is still a wolf. The powers we notice are therefore those possessed by their wild ancestors.

Of all our pets' supposed powers, the most extraordinary involve journeys of reunion. In the classic case an owner loses a pet while on holiday, or through it being stolen, or by giving it away to another person. Whatever the method of separation, the pet eventually finds its way back home over journeys that may involve hundreds of kilometres of travel.

In Australia the long-distance record is held by a collie named Whisky. In October 1973, he became parted from his truck-driver owner at a roadside café near Darwin. In July the following year he turned up in his home in Melbourne, after a journey of almost 2900 kilometres.

The British speed record is held by a tabby named McCavity who returned from his new home in Cumbernauld, Scotland, to his old one in Truro, Cornwall, in just three weeks. To make the 800-kilometre journey he must have averaged around 25 miles a day. And there are innumerable similar examples.

Inevitably, some of these travels can be explained by mistaken identity; a person who has lost a beloved cat is only too willing to believe that the emaciated stray on the doorstep is the one that went missing many months ago. But there is a core of reports that, due to certain distinguishing marks on the cat or dog, leave no doubts that the feat has been achieved. In many ways, this should not surprise us – each weekend thousands of racing pigeons are released far from home and make similar incredible journeys.

Experiments have been conducted in which cats were taken on car journeys to disorientate them and then they were released into a maze with twenty-four different exits. Results showed that they generally set off in the correct direction right from the start. In similar tests, cats competed against pigeons and showed a superior ability to orientate correctly.

Like birds, cats and dogs are likely to use a variety of cues to guide them as they travel. The most important of these involves knowing where their release point is in relation to home. How this is achieved is still a mystery. It might involve memorizing the twists and turns of the outward journey, but this idea has been largely disproven; the most favoured explanation involves sensing changes in the magnetic field at the new location.

Assuming that an animal makes the right choice when it sets off, the rest of the journey involves maintaining the correct course. As we saw in Chapter 4, many animals use the sun as a guide to direction, employing an accurate time sense to compensate for its movements across the sky. They also use the stars; the pole star and the constellations that revolve around it can be unerring night-time guides. The earth's magnetic field acts as a back-up system, giving compass cues even when heavy clouds obscure the sky.

How many of these aids are used by cats or dogs is unknown. But once they reach the general vicinity of home, their sense of smell must certainly be brought into play. In both pets this sense is highly developed and it is likely that the odours of home guide them on the final stages of their journey. These smells can carry many kilometres on the breeze. Even birds, such as pigeons, not known for their remarkable sense of smell, construct a smell map of their local area that helps guide them home from some distance away. It must be far easier for a dog or a cat to perform these feats.

There is a second kind of homing, less easily explained by our present understanding of animal navigation, and that is when a pet, left behind when an owner moves away, somehow finds its way to the new location. The only explanations that fit the current framework of scientific belief involve cases of mistaken identity or chance encounters. But this side-steps the question and some people propose that there must be a connection between a pet and its owner, not yet understood by science, that can somehow straddle vast distances. This would certainly explain how easy it seems to be for animals to find each other in the wild. It would also account for another puzzling pet phenomenon: how they seem to know when their owners are about to arrive home.

Dolphin therapy. People greet a dolphin in an encounter group, convinced of the dolphin's Super-Natural healing powers.

Pet Precognition

Many people report that their pet anticipates their arrival by appearing expectantly at the window. Because a dog or cat's time sense is known to be incredibly precise a person returning from work or making other regular journeys can easily be anticipated, but some animals seem to react to less predictable appearances. The most likely explanation is that their acute sense of hearing is keyed into sounds of which we are largely unaware. Keys jangling in the distance create ultrasonic signals that the cat's ear, tuned to sounds three times higher than ours, may be able to hear. A car engine may make distinctive ultrasonic noises and human footsteps may also have their own distinguishing characteristics.

Cats and dogs are also highly selective to any sounds that may be significant to them. They ignore most of the babble of our conversation, but key words such as 'walk', 'food' or 'bed' evoke an immediate response. A can of pet food being opened is an even more effective trigger. The same selective hearing, directed at a returning owner, may account for many of the reported incidents.

Pet Healing

Pets possess yet another near SuperNatural power of which much has been made in recent years. Tests involving children and the elderly show that pets have the power to heal.

There is no question about the health benefits of keeping pets. People who do so seem to suffer from less stress and enjoy better health than those without these companions. This particularly applies to people living on their own. Cats and dogs fit into our world so easily because they are social animals. The dog in particular comes from a social world very similar to our own – the wolf pack is a mirror of the small family groups that made up early human hunter-gatherers, and the same bonds of friendship and affection held both groups together. Taken into our world, the dog simply transfers this affection to us, providing a perfect human substitute for lonely people. The cat, although less unreservedly devoted, shows similar affection. Being wanted and needed brings obvious health benefits.

It has been shown in various studies that patients recovering from a heart attack are more likely to survive if they have a pet as a companion. The mere act of stroking a cat or dog lowers blood pressure and heart rate and seems to bring similar benefits to that given by meditation.

Because of the health benefits they bring, pets are now being used in many hospitals to help patients recuperate faster. By promoting a general feeling of well-being they speed recovery. They also bring other benefits; they give a patient something to care for and so help reverse the feeling of dependency that hospitals engender.

Pets' healing powers work particularly well for those with mental health problems, providing a lifeline back to reality. For people who find it difficult to make social attachments, having a pet gives them a chance to give love with no strings attached. They will accept affection from a pet long before they accept it from another person. Because of pets' unconditional attachment they also seem to stifle aggression.

The fact that we can understand the healing powers of pets through the current knowledge of science should not make them any less wonderful, but there seems to be something in the human psyche that devalues a puzzle once it has been explained. We cherish mysteries, and none more so than those surrounding dolphins.

SuperNatural Dolphins

Dolphins have overtaken all other animals as representatives of the SuperNatural. One of the most intriguing recent developments is their apparently magical ability to heal certain kinds of illnesses. Patients meet these intelligent marine mammals in encounter sessions and come away from the meetings improved in health. It has been claimed that dolphins help people with disabilities such as Down's syndrome, autism and muscular dystrophy. They also seem to boost the production of the brain's natural opiates, endorphins, and the increase infection-fighting T-cells that help people with cancer or AIDS. In one much publicized case, an eight-year-old English boy, trapped in a world of silence since birth, uttered his first words after spending three days in dolphin therapy.

There is little doubt that an encounter with dolphins can improve the health of some people, particularly those suffering from clinical depression. The debate concerns the method. The most sceptical scientists suggest that simply the excitement of meeting such a large, charismatic animal at close hand is enough to induce a feeling of euphoria in susceptible people and, coupled with the holiday that surrounds the experience, health benefits inevitably follow. Others look for a deeper reason.

The most fascinating hypothesis concerns the power of the sonar that dolphins use to scan people in the water. Focused by the bump on the dolphin's head known as the melon, these high-energy ultrasonic emissions can stun fish by making their swim bladders resonate. People swimming with dolphins sometimes feel themselves being 'zapped' by these sound beams, resulting in a strange tingling sensation. One theory suggests that the dolphin's sonar may affect body tissue at a cellular level. Intriguingly, ultrasound is used by physiotherapists as a means of treating damaged tissue, although the frequencies used are five times higher pitched than those employed by dolphins. These ideas are still being investigated by science.

People who promote the idea of dolphin healing tend to suggest that these are magical mammals with some great affinity for humans, imbued with almost mystic powers. They also suggest that dolphins have never been known to attack humans and that there is some great psychic bond between us. In truth, although dolphins are remarkable animals with an apparent affinity for us, if males were used more regularly in therapy sessions there would be plenty of nips and casualties. The bite marks that decorate most dolphins' bodies are testament to an aggressive side that is rarely talked about.

In dolphin therapy, our quest for the SuperNatural meets the cutting edge of scientific research; as a result there is fierce debate and great scepticism as to what is really happening. Hard science reveals that dolphins have the power to gain a view of us that is far outside normal human experience. Just as their sonar can penetrate our bodies and 'see' the outline of our skeleton (see Chapter 1, page 48), so they also have the means to detect cancers by noticing the changes in density of body tissue. They are capable of sensing metal pins in legs and joints or the pacemaker in a heart patient's body. They may even investigate these strange objects. Whether they are likely to do anything with the information is where science and faith diverge. This inevitably happens at the edge of scientific understanding. Science is the only tool we have to make sense of the world, but where there are gaps in understanding, the human imagination works hard to plug them.

However much science explains mysteries, there always seem to be new ones to uncover. Few people now believe that it will ever be possible to know everything and so the natural world will always retain some enigmas. We seem to prefer it that way. Our earliest relationship with the natural world was a SuperNatural one; the cave paintings of Lascaux, the Nasca Lines of Peru and the practices of the few tribal shamans that have survived to the present day all suggest a basic human desire to reach out and touch the unexplained. Although today science has pushed back the boundaries of knowledge, enough unanswered questions still remain to satisfy that human need. Perhaps this is the way it should always be.